TRADITIONAL
SCOTTISH
RECIPES

WAVERLEY BOOKS

Some hae meat and canna eat,
And some wad eat that want it,
We hae meat and we can eat,
And sae the Lord be thankit.

'The Selkirk Grace'
Attributed to Robert Burns

With love and thanks to everyone whose family recipes appear in this book:

Margaret Cowan
John Cowan
Jean Brownlee
Isa Brownlee
Jimmy Brownlee
Robert Purdie

Eleanor Purdie
Margaret Hammond
Margaret Irvine
Barbara Browning
Jean Thomson
Tam Brownlee

Published 2018 by Waverley Books, an imprint of
The Gresham Publishing Company Ltd, Academy Park, Building 4000,
Gower Street, Glasgow, G51 1PR, Scotland

First published 2009. Reprinted 2010, 2014 (twice), 2015,
2016 (twice), 2017, 2018 (twice).

Copyright © 2014 The Gresham Publishing Company

Text by Eleanor Cowan
Previously published as *Traditional Scottish Cookery*
by Lomond Books

Line drawings by Toni Goffe of Linda Rogers Associates
Pheasant, page 101, by Mark Mechan
Cover by Mark Mechan
Other illustrations by Elizabeth Sawyer and
Carol Daniel of Simon Girling and Associates

ISBN 978 1 902407 77 7
Printed and bound in the EU

CONTENTS

BREAKFAST DISHES

FISH AND SEAFOOD

SOUPS

SAVOURY DISHES

MEAT AND GAME

DESSERTS

CAKES, BISCUITS AND TEA BREADS

CHITTERIN' BITES

JAMS AND PRESERVES

DRINKS

Weights and Measures

Measurements

1 cm = 10 mm

Inches	Centimetres
1/8	0.3
1/4	0.6
2/5 (0.39)	1
1/2	1.3
3/4	2
1	2.5
2	5
3	7.6
4	10
5	12.7
6	15.2
7	17.8
8	20.3
9	22.8
10	25.4
11	28
12	30.5

Temperatures

Gas Mark	°F	°C
	32	0
	50	10
	100	40
	122	50
	212	100
1	275	140
2	300	150
3	325	160
4	350	180
5	375	190
6	400	200
7	425	220
8	450	230
9	475	250

Weights

Imperial	Metric
0.35 oz	10 g
1/2 oz	14 g
3/4 oz	21 g
1 oz	28 g
1 1/2 oz	43 g
2 oz	57 g
2 1/2 oz	71 g
3 oz	85 g

Weight

Imperial	Metric
4 oz	113 g
4 1/2 oz	127 g
5 oz	141 g
6 oz	170 g
7 oz	198 g
8 oz (1/2 lb)	226 g
9 oz	255 g
10 oz	283 g
12 oz	340 g
1 lb	453 g
1 1/2 lbs	680 g
2 lbs	900 g
2.3 lbs	1 kg
3 lbs	1.360 kg

Volume

1 pint = 20 fl oz = 32 tbsps
1/2 pint = 10 fl oz = 16 tbsps
1/4 pint = 5 fl oz = 8 tbsps
1 litre = 1000 ml

Imperial	Metric
2 fl oz	55 ml
3 fl oz	75 ml
5 fl oz	150 ml
10 fl oz	275 ml
15 fl oz (3/4)	425 ml
scant 1 pint	500 ml
1 pint	570 ml
1 1/4 pint	725 ml
1 3/4 pint	1 litre
2 pints	1.2 litres
2 1/4 pints	1.5 litres

Cups

Cup measures should be used in proportion to each other. Use the same cup for each measurement.

1 cup flour	= 4 oz
1 cup butter	= 8 oz
1 cup sugar	= 8 oz
1 cup icing sugar	= 5 oz
1 cup breadcrumbs	= 3 oz
1 cup grated cheese	= 4 oz
1 cup dry rice	= 7 oz
1 cup syrup	= 13 oz

American Measurements

In the recipes, measurements are given with metric measures first followed by conversions to UK imperial measurements.

UK imperial	metric	US
1 oz flour	25 g	quarter cup
4 oz flour	125 g	one cup
8 oz flour	250 g	two cups
2 oz breadcrumbs (fresh)	60 g	one cup
4 oz breadcrumbs (dry)	125 g	one cup
4 oz oatmeal	125 g	one cup (scant)
5 oz currants	150 g	one cup
4 oz shredded suet	125 g	one cup (scant)
4 oz butter and other fats, including cheese	125 g	one stick
8 oz butter and other fats, including grated cheese	250 g	one cup
7 oz caster/granulated sugar	200 g	one cup
8 oz caster/granulated sugar	250 g	one and a quarter cups
8 oz meat (chopped/minced/ground)	250 g	One cup
8 oz cooked, mashed potatoes	250 g	One cup

tbsp	= tablespoon
tsp	= teaspoon
1 oz	= 1 rounded tbsp
1 tbsp of liquid	= 3 tsps
1 tsp liquid	= 5 ml
1 British tsp	= 1 American tsp
1 British tbsp liquid	= 17.7 ml
1 US tbsp liquid	= 14.2 ml
8 tbsps	= 4 fl oz = 125 ml = half cup
8 fl oz	= 250 ml = 1 cup (half a US pint)
1/2 pint/10 fl oz	= 300 ml = 1 1/4 cups (scant)
3/4 pint/15 fl oz	= 450 ml = 2 cups (scant) or 1 US pint
1 British pint/20 fl oz	= 600 ml = 2 1/2 cups

UK terms	US terms
Ingredients	
bacon rashers	bacon slices
bannock	flat round cake
bicarbonate of soda	baking soda
biscuits	crackers/cookies
boiling fowl	stewing fowl
cake mixture	cake batter
caster sugar	granulated sugar
celery stick	celery stalk
cornflour	cornstarch
chips	french fried potatoes
creamed potatoes	mashed potatoes
crisps	potato chips
demerara sugar	light brown sugar
dessicated coconut	flaked coconut
digestive biscuits	Graham crackers
double cream	heavy cream
essence	extract (in the UK extract is a purer form of flavouring than essence, e.g. vanilla essence and vanilla extract)
farls	quarters
fats	shortening
flaked almonds	slivered almonds
glacé	candied
golden syrup	light corn syrup
hough	shank of beef
icing	frosting
icing sugar	powdered sugar
jam	preserves, jelly
jelly	Jello
mince/minced beef	ground beef
mixed spice	allspice
nub or nut of butter	pat of butter
pinhead oatmeal	irish oatmeal
rasher	slice
ratafia biscuits	almond flavoured cookies/dried macaroons
roast potatoes	oven browned potatoes
scone	shortcake, biscuit
self-raising flour	all-purpose flour with baking powder
single cream	light cream
soft brown sugar	light brown sugar
spring onion	scallion/green onion
stewing steak	braising beef
strong plain flour	unbleached white flour
sultanas	seedless white raisins
treacle	molasses
unsalted butter	sweet butter
wholemeal	wholewheat

UK terms	US terms
Utensils and Methods	
ashet	meat dish, pie dish
baking sheet or tray	cookie sheet
case	pie shell
fry	pan fry (with fat)
frying pan	skillet
girdle	griddle
grate	shred
greaseproof paper	vegetable parchment or waxed paper
grill	broil
gut	clean
knead	punch down
knock back	punch down
liquidiser	electric blender
mince	grind
polythene	plastic wrap
prove	rise
pudding cloth	cheesecloth
roasting tin	roasting pan with rack
sandwich tins	round-layer pans
sieve	sift
stewpan or pan	kettle
tartlet tin	muffin pan
whisk	beat/whip

BREAKFAST DISHES

ARBROATH SMOKIES

Smokies are just as tasty cold with salad as they are hot with buttered toast. Smokies are haddocks, but unlike Finnan haddies they are smoked closed, tied in pairs by their tails. The fish have their heads removed, are gutted and are then dipped in salted water and hung on wooden poles over smouldering wood chips. The process originates from the fishing village of Auchmithie, near Arbroath. The new harbour of Arbroath, established in the 1880s, became the new home of the fishing community of Auchmithie and, as they moved their families there, they brought with them their fish-curing skills. By the beginning of the twentieth century the Smokie industry was well and truly established in Arbroath.

1 pair of smokies
Butter

Preheat the oven to 180°C/350°F/gas mark 4, or you could use a medium-hot grill. Remove the backbone from each smokie by placing each on a flat surface, skin side down, and press along the length of the bone to help loosen it from the flesh. You should now be able to remove the bone whole. Smear the smokies with butter and place on a tray in the oven or under the grill for around 15 to 20 minutes. Serve with hot, buttered toast. Serves two for breakfast.

KEDGEREE

This breakfast dish, with a hint of spice and delicious moist, flaked Scottish Finnan haddies, is definitely a meeting of culinary cultures.

> 6 tbsps long grain rice
> 2 Finnan haddies
> 60 g/2 oz butter
> 4 hard boiled eggs
> Lemon juice
> ½ tsp cayenne pepper (curry powder is an alternative included in Mrs Beeton's recipe)
> Pinch of salt
> Chopped parsley

Boil the rice in salted water. Poach the haddock, remove the bones and flake the fish. Melt the butter in a large saucepan and add the flaked fish, rice, lemon juice and seasoning. Heat through but do not stir too strongly or you will reduce the flakes of fish to mush. Chop the eggs and either mix through the rice or dish up the rice and fish and sprinkle them on the top. Garnish with chopped parsley. Serves four to six people.

BAPS

These baps, or morning rolls, are the perfect accompaniment to a hearty breakfast.

450 g/1 lb strong plain white flour
2 level tsps salt
50 g/2 oz vegetable fat or butter
15 g/½ oz dried yeast
1 tsp caster sugar
125 ml/¼ pint milk
125 ml/¼ pint tepid water

Sieve the flour and salt, and rub in the fat. Mix together the yeast, caster sugar and water. Heat the milk until it is lukewarm and then add it to the yeast mixture. Gradually add the liquid to the flour and knead to a soft dough for about ten minutes, or until you feel the dough becoming elastic. Place in an oiled bowl and cover with cling film. Leave the bowl in a warm place for an hour, or in a cool place overnight.

Turn the dough out of the bowl, knead it lightly and divide into around seven ovals. Place them on a greased baking tray, cover and leave to prove in a warm place for a further 30 minutes.

Brush with milk and dust with flour and place in the oven at 220ºC/425ºF/gas mark 7, for 15 to 20 minutes Eat warm with butter and Dundee marmalade.

BUTTERIES

Butteries or 'Buttery Rowie' rolls were associated with the Aberdonian fishing fleets. Their charm today is their superbly unfashionable high fat content and they are absolutely delicious hot with butter and with both savoury and sweet toppings.

> 450 g/1 lb plain flour
> 20 g/¾ oz fresh yeast
> 20 g/¾ oz caster sugar
> 220 g/8 oz soft white fat or butter
> 110 g/4 oz lard or solid vegetable
>   fat
> 250 ml/½ pint tepid water

Sieve the flour onto your work surface. Dissolve the sugar in the water and then crumble the yeast into the water and mix thoroughly. Make a well in the centre of the flour into which you should pour some of the liquid. Gradually mix the liquid with the flour using a fork. Once all of the liquid is combined with the flour, knead the mixture using your hands. Knead the dough until it is smooth and elastic in consistency. Score the dough with a cross and place in a bowl in a warm place to prove for around 1 hour. The dough should double in size.

Knead the dough again, briefly and very lightly.

Mix together the two fats with a hand blender or cream them together with a wooden spoon.

Roll out the dough. Spread the top two thirds of the dough lightly with one third of the fat. Fold the bottom third up over the middle and then fold the top third over. Leave in the refrigerator for 30 minutes and repeat the process another twice with the rest of the fat, but turn the dough so that you are not applying the fat to the same areas each time. Leave the dough to rest in a cool place after each rolling. Divide the dough into approximately 15 ovals and place on greased, floured baking trays, leaving space for them to rise. Bake at 200°C/400°F/gas mark 6, for 20 to 25 minutes until golden brown and risen.

Makes around fifteen butteries.

SCRAMBLED EGGS AND SMOKED SCOTTISH SALMON

An absolutely delicious and slightly indulgent breakfast dish that's perfect for a romantic weekend. Even though you will be cutting the smoked salmon into quite thin strips, buy quality smoked salmon slices rather that the packets of smoked salmon pieces that are available in the supermarket. These pieces can be tough, bony and rather unpleasant. Not what you want for your romantic breakfast! Also don't be tempted to use milk instead of cream. If you prefer to cook your eggs to a very firm consistency the milk will separate from the eggs leaving a runny liquor that you'll have to drain off. As cream is almost entirely fat-based it won't separate from the eggs and you can have them as firm as you like, at twice the calories mind you, but then, you wouldn't eat this every day.

> 3 large free-range eggs
> 2 tbsps double cream
> 25 g/1 oz butter
> 25 g/1 oz best Scottish smoked
>   salmon, thinly sliced

Beat the eggs in a bowl and whisk in the double

cream. Slowly melt the butter in a small non-stick saucepan over a medium heat. Add the eggs and cook until they are just beginning to firm up, or longer if you find runny eggs unappetising. Add the thinly sliced pieces of smoked salmon and remove from the heat. You don't want to cook the smoked salmon, merely allow it to be heated through by the eggs. Serve immediately with buttered toast.

Serves two.

PORRIDGE

Porridge is one of the healthiest ways to start the day. Oats is an energy-giving superfood, and despite Dr Johnson's derision that it was 'a grain which in England is generally given to horses but in Scotland supports the people', porridge will fill you up from early morning right through till the afternoon. So, more fool the doctor.

Porridge, confusingly referred to in the plural as 'they' (referring to the oats), would traditionally (genuinely!) have been poured into a drawer in the kitchen, left to cool and cut into slices for the men to take to work. It might also have been fried and served with eggs for dinner.

It should be made with coarse or pinhead oatmeal, rather than rolled oats, to be authentically Scottish. If you want to be totally authentic, the milk that accompanies porridge should not be poured over it but poured into a separate bowl and each spoonful of porridge cooled in the bowl of milk. This ensures the milk stays as cold as possible. And of course 'they' should only be seasoned with salt. In truth, it's safe to claim that perfectly traditional additions to porridge would be honey or treacle. But the addition of salt to oats really brings out its flavour, so be sure to include a good pinch of salt no matter what sweet topping you prefer.

1 cup of coarse or pinhead oatmeal
3 cups of cold water
Salt

Soak the oatmeal overnight (if you are using rolled oats then there is no need to do this). The following day, add a good pinch of salt and bring the oatmeal slowly to the boil. Stir continuously with a wooden spoon and serve when thick and creamy. Serve with full-cream milk and a further sprinkling of salt (or the sweet topping of your choice).

Serves two.

FISH AND SEAFOOD

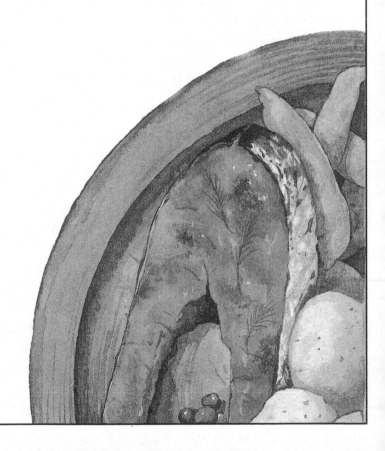

GRILLED CLABBY DOOS

Clabbies are large mussels native to Scotland. You should prepare them as you would normal mussels, rather than trying to open them uncooked. You should plunge them into boiling water and of course discard any that fail to open.

Two slices of white bread
2 tbsps Scottish cheddar cheese, grated
2 tbsp chopped chives
1 tbsp chopped parsley
6 Clabby Doos

Tear up the bread and, using a food processor, turn it into breadcrumbs. Chop the chives and parsley finely and process these briefly with the crumbs. In a bowl, mix the crumbs with the cheese. Put the clabbies in a pan of boiling salted water and cook for 3 to 5 minutes or until the mussels open. Shaking the pan will help them to open up.

Remove the clabbies from the pot and remove one half shell from each and discard. Remove the tough chewy ring that surrounds the meat. Top each one with the breadcrumb mixture and place under a medium grill until golden brown on top.

Serves two as a starter.

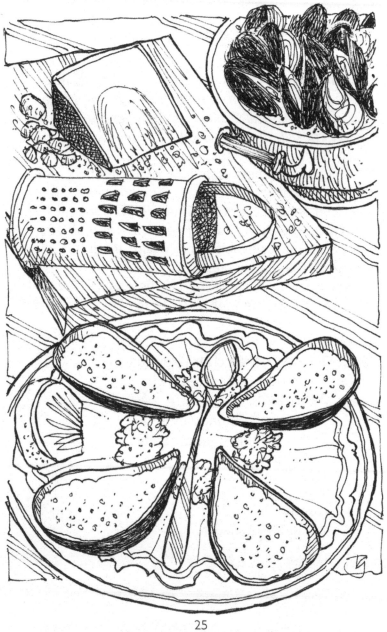

DRESSED CRAB

Making dressed crab is a lot of work especially if you have to cook them from fresh. And by fresh I mean ... alive. Thankfully most fishmongers sell them ready-cooked, thus relieving you of the need to boil something alive (something even the most carnivorous amongst us find frankly off-putting). The recommended way of cooking fresh crustaceans is to freeze them into unconsciousness in your freezer for 2 hours. Then slowly bring them to the boil after which you boil them vigorously with the lid on the pan for 10 to 20 minutes.

Now, having put this murderous episode behind us, we can assume that the crab is already cooked and get on with the recipe.

1 large cooked crab (around
   1.3 kg/3 lb in weight)
2 tbsps single cream
½ cup white breadcrumbs
Two hard-boiled eggs, finely
   chopped
1 tsp mustard
Salt
Pepper
Chopped parsley

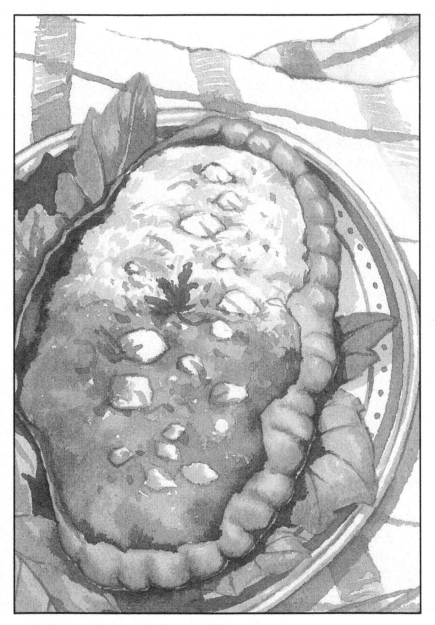

Place the crab on its back on a large chopping board. Twist off a claw, steadying the body of the crab with your other hand. Hold the claw close to its body as you do so. Remove the other claw and the legs in the same way.

Snap the claws in half at the joint, and then, using a hammer, tap the claws open on their rounded sides. Remove the white meat from the claws. Use a small knife or a teaspoon to make sure that you collect all of the meat. Do the same to the larger of the legs and remove the white meat. With the crab on its back and its tail flap towards you, press the body section away from the shell by forcing your fingers upwards from beneath the body flap and easing it out of its shell. You will notice grey, feather-like gills. Discard these as they are inedible. Also discard the stomach bag and mouth which are attached to the back shell. Run a knife around the shell to help loosen the brown meat and bring it out smoothly. Place in a bowl and clean out the shell, throwing away the membrane. Remove the rest of the inner shell of the crab by tapping with a hammer. Thoroughly scrub the shell as it will be used to serve the brown and white meat. Cut the body of the crab in two and scoop out the brown meat which you will place in the bowl with the rest of the brown meat. Throw away the rest of the body.

Cream the brown meat with the cream,

breadcrumbs and seasoning. Finely chop the hard-boiled eggs and mix with the parsley. Place the white meat on one side of the shell and the brown meat on the other and sprinkle the chopped eggs and parsley over the top. Serve with salad, crusty bread and butter or even oatcakes. One large crab should serve three to four as a starter.

POACHED FINNAN HADDIES

Finnan or Findon haddock are named after the town of Findon near Aberdeen where this method of smoking fish was a speciality.

The haddies are filleted, dipped in salt water, hung up to dry and then smoked over peat or sawdust until they become golden brown in colour. Haddies poached in milk are a lovely and very simple tea-time dish.

> 2 fillets of Finnan haddock (smoked haddock)
> Around 250 ml/½ pint milk or enough to almost cover the fish in your pan
> Freshly ground black pepper
> 25 g/1 oz butter

To a large frying pad add milk, ground pepper, a knob of butter and the haddies. Bring the ingredients slowly to the boil and cook until the flesh whitens and becomes tender.

Serve with some of the poached milk with wholemeal soda bread and butter or floury potatoes.

Serves two.

FISH PIE

This is a simple and delicious way of eating Scottish haddock and is a very handy dish that can be made the night before and heated up the following day.

2 slices filleted haddock
1 slice smoked haddock
A little milk for poaching
5 potatoes, boiled and mashed
25 g/1 oz butter
3 hard-boiled eggs, chopped
Bechamel sauce:
  1 tbsp butter
  1 tbsp plain flour
  500 ml/1 pint milk

Poach the fish in milk and flake into small pieces. Hard-boil the eggs and chop finely. Boil and mash the potatoes with butter and milk or cream. Make a simple white (bechamel) sauce: melt the butter in a saucepan and mix with a little flour; gradually mix in the milk and bring to the boil in order to cook the raw flour; add more milk if you find the sauce to be too thick. Gently fold in the flaked fish and chopped boiled eggs. Pour into a casserole dish and top with the mashed potato. Bake in a hot oven until the potato topping turns golden brown.
  Serves two.

TROUT WITH ALMONDS

Trout could traditionally have been eaten coated in oats like the herring recipe (page 40). This recipe using almonds would have been a slightly more indulgent way of eating fish, as oats were a staple that everyone could afford whereas almonds were a luxury.

2 250-g/½-lb trouts
2 tbsp plain flour with salt and
   pepper seasoning
Cooking oil
Butter
50 g/2 oz flaked almonds
The juice of half a lemon

Wash and dry the trout then roll them in the seasoned flour. Heat some butter and the oil in a frying pan over a medium heat and then fry the fish for around 5 to 7 minutes on each side. Remove from the pan but keep warm. To a clean pan (wipe clean with kitchen roll rather that wash) add some more butter and melt over a moderate heat. Add the almonds to the pan and turn up the heat to fry them until they are brown. Dish up the hot trout, and squeeze a little lemon juice over each fish.

Cover the fish with the toasted almonds and serve with creamed potatoes and green beans.

Serves two.

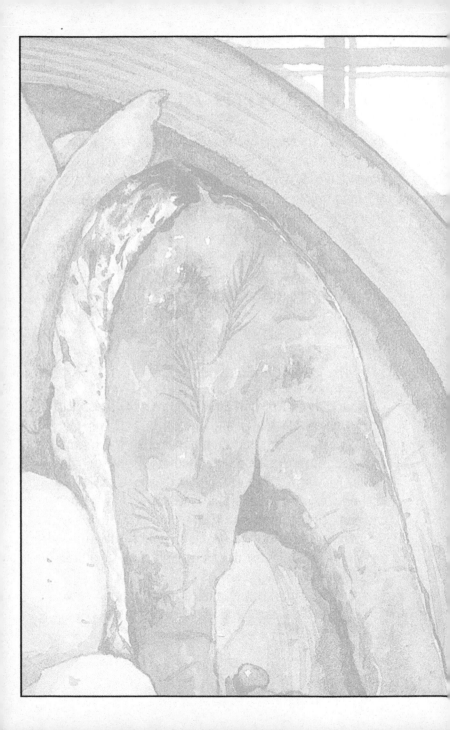

GRILLED SCOTTISH SALMON STEAK

This is a very simple way of eating one of Scotland's finest exports. Wild Scottish salmon is best, if you can get it.

Wild Scottish salmon steak about
    4 cm/1 ½ inches thick
Vegetable oil
25 g/1 oz butter, melted
Chopped parsley
Chopped dill
Lemon juice

Dip the steak in melted butter or vegetable oil, sprinkle with salt and place under a hot grill until the flesh changes colour. Turn the steak and cook the other side. Serve with the central bone removed.

For a sauce, melt a little butter, add dill, parsley, a squeeze of lemon juice and pour around the steak. Serve with boiled potatoes and shelled or sugar-snap peas.

Serves one.

FRIED HADDOCK WITH CHIPS AND MARROWFAT PEAS

Some have said that fish and chips kept the nation going during the second world war (fish and potatoes were not rationed during the war). Fresh haddock is, despite being deep-fried, actually full of more nutrients than it is given credit for. However, the main reason for eating a fish supper is undoubtedly not for good health. Is there anyone alive who can resist that chip shop smell? The Scottish fish supper has always been made with haddock (the English with cod) and this recipe aims to capture the crispiness of the batter from good chip shop fish. The chips, however, are decidedly home-made in style and should be made with golden wonder potatoes if you can get your hands on them (local farmers are your best bet). If they are not golden wonder you can parboil the potatoes before frying to help make them more floury (though they will absorb more oil).

The batter recipe is Margaret Irvine's, who makes the best fritters.

The peas:
300 g/10 oz dried marrowfat peas
Malt vinegar (enough to moisten
   the soaked peas)
Salt

The batter:
Self-raising flour
Soda water or sparkling mineral
    water
Malt vinegar
A pinch of salt

Four fillets of fresh haddock (good
    quality frozen fresh haddock is
    also fine)
4 or 5 floury potatoes depending
    on their size (and depending on
    how many chips you think you
    can eat)

Soak the dried peas overnight. The next evening
cover them with boiling water and boil for around
an hour. Test them to see if they are tender. Drain
them but retain just a tiny bit of the water to keep
them moist. Add as much vinegar as suits your
taste and season with salt.

Peel the potatoes and cut them into large chips.
Parboil them for around 5 minutes or so.
Afterwards, drain and place in a tea towel to
ensure that most of the moisture is absorbed

Sieve the flour into a bowl and add a pinch of
salt. Make a well in the centre and add the fizzy
water gradually, whisking it with a metal fork or
a balloon whisk until the batter reaches a smooth,

thick but creamy consistency and shows bubbles on the surface. At this stage you can add 2 tbsps of malt vinegar which helps to add to the batter's crispiness.

Heat some oil in a deep fat fryer. If there is not a temperature gauge on your fryer you can test the fat with a small spoonful of batter. If it quickly hardens and turns yellow then the fat is hot enough. Preheat your oven to high. Dry the haddock fillet with kitchen roll, then dip it in the batter and coat it thoroughly. Immediately place it in the fryer. The fish will take between 5 and 10 minutes to cook. Don't let it get too brown. Remove from the fryer, dry on kitchen roll and keep warm in the oven. Do the same with the rest of the haddock fillets and fry the chips till golden brown.

Serve immediately. Serves four.

HERRING IN OATMEAL

This is yet another traditional Scottish dish that is simple, cheap and thoroughly delicious. Herring can be served for breakfast, with toast and tea, or dinner, complemented by boiled new potatoes and green beans. They are also delicious made with mustard sauce.

4 filleted, boned herrings
Enough medium oatmeal to coat
 the fish
Salt
Pepper
Butter

Wash the fish in cold water. Season a plateful of oatmeal and press each side of the fish in it firmly to coat each side completely. Melt a generous knob of butter in a frying pan, taking care not to burn the butter, and fry the fillets of fish, two at a time, for around 3 minutes on each side. Fry the fish skin side down first so that they do not break into pieces. Place the fillets on a plate under a hot grill until you have fried them all.

Serve with new potatoes and green vegetables. Serves two.

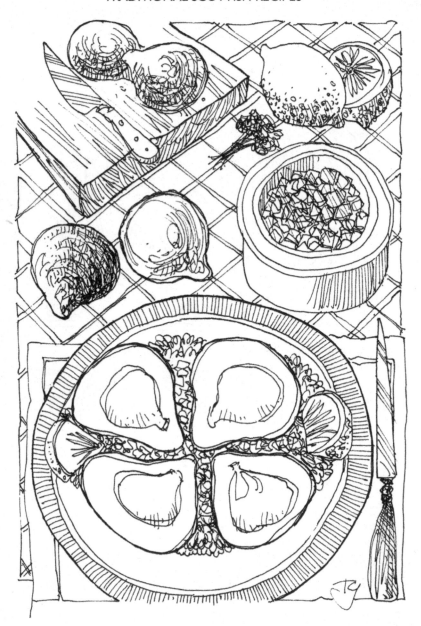

NATIVE SCOTTISH OYSTERS

Not so long ago, the oyster was not considered a luxury foodstuff. These shellfish were cheap and plentiful only one hundred years ago and could be enjoyed by everyone. They would have been used as the contents of pies and stews and as stuffing for roasts. Pollution and overfishing have destroyed many oyster beds on the coastline of Scotland and oysters are now a rare and expensive item.

It seems rather a waste to risk cooking them. That is why this 'recipe' is for raw oysters. This is not exactly a traditional Scottish way of eating them, but personally, I am too mean to put them in a stew. The best Scottish oysters for eating raw are native oysters, but if you can't get hold of these – and they are expensive – rock oysters are farmed all year round at Loch Fyne and are a bit more affordable and perfectly tasty.

> 6 native Scottish oysters (*Ostrea edulis*)
> Enough ice to fill your serving dish
> 1 lemon cut into small wedges

When buying live oysters you should ensure that you choose ones where the shells are firmly shut. They can be kept in the refrigerator for two days.

Place them deep shell downwards in a bowl and cover them with a damp cloth. You might think that covering them in cold water would be a good idea but in fact it is not, and on no account should they be fed. Scrub the shells thoroughly.

Opening the oysters: hold the oyster, cup side down, in a gloved hand or with a thick cloth. Using an oyster knife (short, pointed, strong and thick-bladed) prize open the oyster at the hinge by pushing and twisting simultaneously. Then run the knife under the top shell to sever the muscle. Carefully run the knife along the entire rim of the shell. Remove the top shell but be careful not to lose too much of the juices from inside. Make sure the flesh is entirely loosened from the shells so that they can be eaten smoothly.

Serve immediately on a bed of ice and eat each one with a small squeeze of lemon.

Serves two as an appetiser.

PRAWNS POACHED IN WINE AND CREAM

Don't choose a cheap wine for this recipe just because it's for cooking with. It needn't be the best there is, but at least choose one that you would be happy drinking on its own.

450 g/1 lb freshly peeled Scottish
   prawns
1 onion
1 clove of garlic, chopped or
   crushed
300 ml/½ pint white wine
25 g/1 oz butter
150 ml/¼ pint double cream
1 tbsp dry pale sherry
Salt and pepper
Chopped parsley and chopped dill

Fry the onions until they are just soft. Pour in the white wine and add the chopped garlic and bring to a slow simmer. Add the prawns and the cream and poach with the lid on the pan for around 10 to 15 minutes. Taste the sauce and season.

If you like, add one tablespoon of dry sherry. Add a generous handful of chopped parsley and a little chopped dill, and serve with bread or floury boiled potatoes. Serves two.

SOUPS

COCK-A-LEEKIE SOUP

After haggis and shortbread, this is probably the next most recognisably Scottish dish. It is an extremely old dish which was enjoyed by the kings of Scotland and working folk alike. The traditional way of making it is to make stock from a whole fresh chicken rather than with leftover chicken bones. In older time it would have been made with an old boiling fowl, a cockerel at the end of its life, and the flesh would have been used in another dish. This version of the recipe includes the addition of sliced prunes. This is a very old tradition and the prunes can of course be left out if they are not to your taste.

1.4-kg/3-lb chicken
1 bay leaf
450 g/1 lb leeks, chopped
2.4 litres/4 pints water
25 g/1 oz rice
100 g/4 oz soaked prunes, sliced
   into strips
Salt and pepper

In a large pot, place the chicken and the giblets (if you have them) the water, bay leaf, the green of the leeks and some salt and pepper. Bring to the boil and then simmer for around 2 to 3 hours. Pierce the flesh of the chicken to make sure it is

cooked. If the flesh is pink, continue to cook. Remove the chicken, giblets and the bay leaf. Remove the green of the leeks if you don't like their slimy texture. Skim any fat from the surface.

Add the rice and cook for 10 minutes. Then add the white of the leeks and the prunes and cook for a further 10 minutes. Remove some flesh from the chicken, add to the soup and cook for a further 10 minutes. Serve garnished with chopped parsley and eat with buttered wholemeal bread.

Makes around six servings.

HARVEST BROTH

This is a delicious, filling and economical soup that would have been certain to keep a working man or woman satisfied.

680 g/1½ lb neck of lamb
225 g/8 oz shelled peas
450 g/4 oz shelled broad beans
   with casing removed
8 spring onions finely chopped
2 carrots
½ turnip chopped
1 small curly kail cabbage
Salt
2.4 litres/4 pints water
2 tbsps chopped parsley

Chop the neck of lamb and trim off the fat. Add the meat to the pan with the water and some salt. Bring the liquid to the boil and skim the surface of fat and other residues. Add the carrots, turnip, peas, beans and onions and boil for one hour. After one hour, add the chopped curly kail and boil for a further 30 minutes. After this, add the chopped parsley and serve.

  Makes around six to eight servings.

LENTIL SOUP

Lentil soup is a complete meal, with vegetables, pulses and shreds of delicious smoked ham hough throughout. Serve with thickly sliced bread.

100g/4 oz lentils
25 g/1 oz vegetable oil
75g/3 oz carrots
50 g/2 oz turnips
1 onion
1 large potato
1 litre/2 pints water
1 ham hough
Black pepper

The night before you make the soup, pour the lentils into a glass bowl and pour over enough boiling water to cover them. Leave overnight. The next day drain the lentils and prepare the vegetables for chopping. Dice the vegetables finely. Pour a little vegetable oil into a large pot and cook the vegetables over a low heat with the lid on for around 20 minutes or until softened, stirring occasionally. Add the water and the ham hough and then bring to the boil. Simmer for around 2 hours, after which you should remove the ham hough and, when cool enough, shred the meat from the bone and add to the soup. Taste and season with black pepper and salt if necessary. If at this point the ham hough has made the soup too salty, you can add a whole potato to the pot and heat the soup until the potato is cooked. This will draw salt from the liquid. You can use this recipe to make pea soup using dried split green or yellow peas instead of lentils.

Makes around six servings.

CULLEN SKINK

A name to perplex tourists. (Cullen is a place in Moray and skink is a Scots word for soup.) Cullen skink can be more like a stew than a soup. When made well, from good smoked fish, it is hearty and utterly delicious.

> 1 onion, sliced or chopped
> 3 or 4 crushed peppercorns
> Butter
> Water
> 1 medium Finnan haddie (salted
>   smoked haddock)
> 450 g/1 lb (approx.) potatoes
> 600 ml/1 pint milk
> Salt and pepper

Fry the onions with some butter and the crushed peppercorns. Add the fish, cover with water and cook until the skin becomes loose enough to remove. Remove the skin and break the fish into flakes, removing the fish bones as you do this. Put the haddock aside and return the skin and bones to the pan and simmer for about an hour to make a stock. Boil and mash the potatoes. Strain the fish stock, add to a large pan and simmer with the milk. Add as much potato as you like, depending on whether you prefer thick or thin soup. Add the flaked haddock. Season with salt, pepper and butter. Serves approximately three to four.

SCOTCH BROTH

Scotch Broth is a great winter soup and is so filling and economical that a pot goes a long way.

> One neck of lamb
> 1.7 litres/3 pints of water
> 25 g/1 oz pearl barley
> 50 g/2 oz dried peas
> 2 carrots, diced
> 1 onion, chopped finely
> 1 leek, sliced
> 1 small turnip, diced
> 100 g/4 oz kail (cabbage), shredded
>   finely
> 1 tbsp parsley, chopped

Soak the peas and barley overnight. The next day, in a pan filled with 1.7 litre/3 pints water, place the lamb, peas, barley and some seasoning and boil for one hour. Skim the surface and then add the carrots, turnip, onion and leek and boil for 15 minutes more. Remove the lamb and flake into small pieces before returning to the pot. Skim off any fat and season if necessary, then serve with chopped parsley.

Makes around six to eight servings.

MUSSEL BREE

This is a rich, tasty, creamy soup-stew. Do remember, before cooking, to discard any mussels that are open, and, after cooking, to discard any that haven't opened.

> 3 dozen mussels in their shells, well
>   scrubbed, beards removed
> 100 g/4 oz chopped leeks
> 50 g/2 oz chopped celery
> 50 g/2 oz chopped onions
> 600 ml/1 pint white wine or dry
>   cider
> 300 ml/½ pint double cream
> 50 g/2 oz butter
> Chopped parsley
> Salt, pepper and grated nutmeg

Scrub the mussels thoroughly; discard any that are open. Bring the vegetables and wine or cider to the boil in a large pan and then drop in the mussels. Cook till they begin to open, then remove from the heat and cover for 10 minutes, shaking the pan occasionally until most have opened. Discard any that remain closed. Remove the mussels. Retain the stock, strain through a fine sieve and return it to the pan.

Set the mussels aside. Taste the stock. Add the cream, butter and parsley and season with salt,

pepper and nutmeg. Add the mussels, in half-shells if you want, and heat them through.

Serve immediately and sprinkle a little chopped, fresh parsley or finely-chopped celery leaves on each portion.

Serves four to six.

TATTIE SOUP

Sometimes the simplest ingredients can make the most delicious combination and this is one instance where this is definitely the case.

2 potatoes
1 small onion
2 rashers Ayrshire bacon
250 ml/½ pt water
1 bay leaf
½ litre/1 pint milk
1 tbsp flour
Salt and pepper
Chopped parsley

Prepare and finely chop or grate the vegetables. Remove the rind from the bacon and cut up finely. Sauté the bacon, potatoes and onion for about 5 minutes. Add the water and bay leaf and boil slowly for 20 minutes. Add the milk, remove the bay leaf and bring to the boil. Blend the flour with a little water and slowly add to the soup, stirring all the time. Finally, season to taste, sprinkle with chopped parsley and serve with wholemeal bread.
  Serves two.

TATTIE AND MUTTON SOUP

The best thing about this delicious and economical soup is the way the sweetness of the grated carrot complements the lamb or mutton.

1 neck, and 1 bone of mutton
2.4 litres/4 pints water (to which
    add 2 tsps salt, ½ tsp white
    pepper, 1 bay leaf, chopped
    carrot, onion and celery)
Salt and pepper
1 kg/2¼ lb peeled potatoes
1 large onion
3 to 4 carrots, peeled and grated
Chopped parsley

Place the neck and bone of mutton in the pot of water. Add seasoning and chopped vegetables and bring to the boil and then simmer for around 1 hour. Remove any scum from the surface of the pot. Strain and reserve the stock and neck. Shred meat from neck of mutton and add to the stock again.

Chop the potatoes and onion finely, grate the carrot, and add them to the pot. Cover and cook for around 30 minutes. Taste the soup and season. Just before serving add the parsley.

Makes around four or five servings.

SAVOURY DISHES

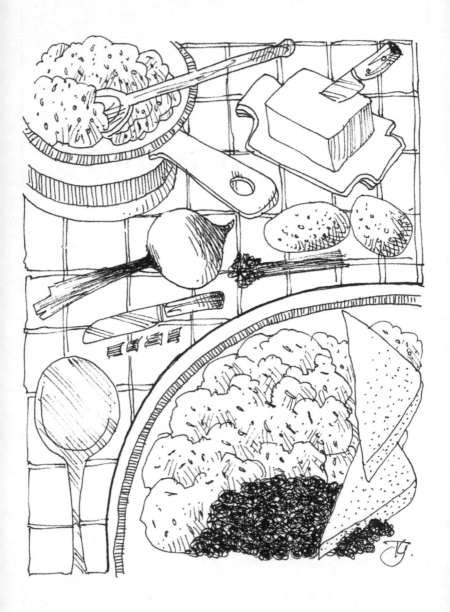

CLAPSHOT

Clapshot is an Orcadian dish (i.e., from the Orkney Isles) and it's possible to make several variations on this theme.

> 450 g/1 lb floury potatoes, boiled
> 450 g/1 lb turnip, chopped and
>   boiled
> 1 onion, fried
> 2 tbsps chopped chives
> Salt and pepper
> 75 g/3 oz butter

Boil the potatoes and turnip. Gently fry the chopped onions in 25 g/1 oz butter until soft but not brown. Mash the boiled potato and boiled turnip together with the remaining butter and the fried onions. Once mashed, mix in the chopped chives and the seasoning.

Serve hot with oatcakes or as an accompaniment to haggis.

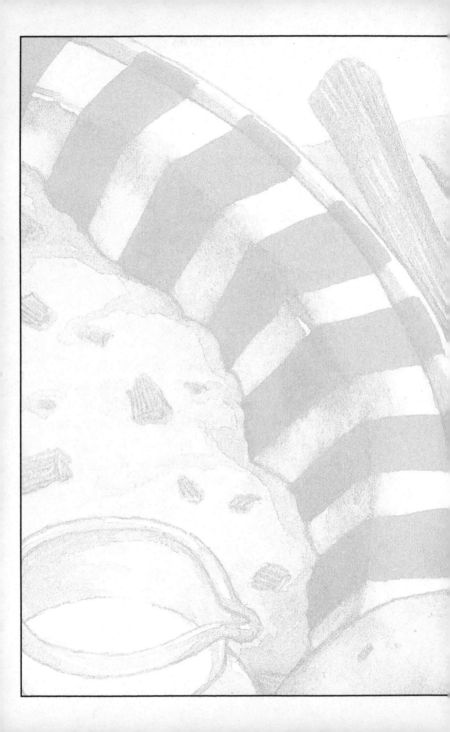

CHAMPIT TATTIES
WITH SPRING ONIONS

A champit tattie is a mashed potato. The relative blandness of mashed potatoes (not the case for all varieties) makes them a perfect vehicle for lots of other stronger flavours. Chopped chives, fried onion, and fried crispy bacon pieces are all particularly tasty additions.

8 medium potatoes (peeled)
Small bunch of spring onions
125 ml/¼ pt milk
Salt and pepper
Knob of butter per person

Boil the potatoes until they are soft. Drain and return them to the heat to dry slightly before mashing. Finely chop the white and green of the spring onions and cook in the milk. Beat this mixture into the mashed potatoes until they are fluffy and smooth. Season to taste and serve a generous helping onto each plate, topping with a knob of butter.

Serves four as a side dish.

RUMBLEDETHUMPS

This delicious dish is the Scottish version of the Irish classic, Colcannon. The recipe is thought to have been brought over from Ireland with the potato in the eighteenth century and it is also known as kailcannon. Kail is a type of cabbage, commonly used in Scottish cookery. As with recipes of this type there are very many versions as it is very much a recipe that can make use of the leftovers from other meals as well as being delicious in its own right. This version originates from the Scottish borders.

If you want, you could also top it with grated cheese.

450 g/1 lb potatoes
4 tbsps single cream
450 g/1 lb cabbage, shredded
Salt and pepper
50 g/2 oz butter
1 tbsp spring onions, chopped
1 tbsp chives, chopped
1 small onion, chopped and fried

Boil the potatoes for around 15 minutes. Shred the cabbage finely and boil until it is just cooked. This should take no more than 5 minutes. Fry the onion until brown and golden but not too crispy. Mash the potatoes till creamy and add the butter

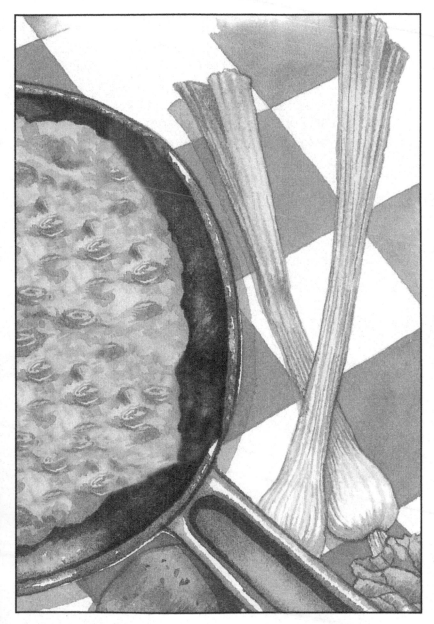

and cream. Mix well with with the cabbage, chopped chives and fried onions. Season well with salt and pepper and taste it. Tip the ingredients into an ovenproof dish. At this point you can put the dish aside to be reheated later or you can bake straight away. You could also cover with grated cheese at this point if desired.

Bake for around 30 minutes until the surface is golden brown.

SKIRLIE

Skirlie is a good accompaniment to game dishes and is also delicious as a stuffing for meat.

> 50 g/2 oz butter or dripping
> 1 onion, chopped
> 100 g/3½ oz medium or coarse
>   oatmeal
> Salt and pepper

Melt the butter or dripping in a frying pan and fry the onion until soft but not too crispy. Then add the oatmeal gradually and stir vigorously until all the fat is absorbed.

Serve hot as an accompaniment to meats or it can be left to cool and used as a stuffing for roasts.

FORFAR BRIDIES

Forfar Bridies are horseshoe shaped, filled with onions and beef, traditionally made with shortcrust suet pastry (rather than puff) and are said to be the best bridies in Scotland. The filling is simply beef and onions so it is important that your two ingredients are of the best quality.

If you wish, you can make pastry in the food processor.

Filling:
450 g/1 lb beef rump, roughly
   minced or chopped
75 g/3 oz grated beef suet
1 onion, finely grated or chopped

Pastry:
300 g/12 oz plain flour
A pinch of salt
75 g/3 oz unsalted butter, diced
75 g/3 oz suet
A little water

Sieve the flour and salt into a bowl and add the cubes of butter and the suet. Rub together with the fingers and bind with a little cold water. A few tablespoons should be enough. Alternatively, throw all the ingredients in a food processor and blend to make a firm dough. Wrap and cool in the fridge for around an hour.

Chop or mince the beef roughly. Grate the onion finely and combine with the chopped beef and suet. Roll out the pastry and divide it into four pieces that are twice as long as they are broad. Place the filling on one half of the pastry, lengthwise, and wet the edges with some water. Fold the remaining pastry over the top and press down firmly around the edges. Trim and make into horseshoe shapes and pinch the pastry around the edges. (Forfar bridies are flat and horseshoe-shaped, rather than shaped like a Cornish pasty which is an upright half moon, crimped on the top.) Make a small slit in the top to let the steam escape while the meat cooks. Place the bridies in the fridge for around half an hour to let the pastry rest. Then place the bridies on a greased baking sheet and bake in an oven preheated to 200°C/400°F/gas mark 6 for between 30 and 40 minutes. Serve hot, straight from the oven.

Makes four.

BACON AND EGG PIE

This is a recipe that my mum has been making for years, and her mother before her. The beauty of it is that you can really use whatever variations of the ingredients you happen to have in the fridge or store cupboard at the time. For this reason it's perfect if you get unexpected dinner guests. It's also exceptionally tasty.

225 g/½ lb Ayrshire bacon
3 eggs
2 dessert apples
100 g/¼ lb cheese
3 tomatoes
Mustard
Rough-puff pastry (easiest to buy
   the ready-rolled or frozen kind
   but, if you like ...)

Rough-puff pastry is a quicker and
   easier version of flaky pastry:
225 g/8 oz plain flour
Pinch of salt
75 g/3 oz butter or margarine, cold
   from the fridge
75 g/3 oz lard
150 ml/¼ pint water

1 tsp lemon juice (do not miss this
   out, it is crucial to the texture of
   the pastry)
Beaten egg

Start by making the pastry, if you have decided to be
brave and make your own. Sieve the flour into a
bowl and add the pinch of salt. Cut the butter and
lard into cubes and, very loosely, mix it with the
flour using a round-bladed knife without breaking
up the pieces of butter. Gradually add the water
(which has 1 tsp lemon juice added to it) and mix
with the knife till it becomes a fairly stiff dough.
Lightly flour a flat surface and roll the dough into
an oblong shape that is three times as long as it is
wide. Fold the bottom third up and the top third
down and seal the sides of the pastry. Chill for 15
minutes. Turn the dough and roll out, fold in the
same way and chill for 15 minutes. Repeat this once
more and them wrap the pastry in greaseproof
paper or cling film and chill for 30 minutes.

Trim off excess fat and fry the Ayrshire bacon,
then chop it into strips. Scramble, or boil and
chop, the eggs. Slice the apples and the tomatoes.
Once all the ingredients are ready to put into the
pie remove the pastry from the fridge. Roll out the
pastry to fit a 20-cm/8-inch sandwich tin, base
and topping. Do this lightly and don't handle the
pastry too much. On the bottom layer of pastry,

spread a little mustard, and on top of this place the slices of apple. On top of the apple slices place the bacon, then the eggs, the tomatoes and finally the grated cheese. Place the pastry top on the pie, crimp at the edges to seal, brush with beaten egg and then score in criss-crosses.

Place in the middle of an oven preheated to 220°C/425°F/gas mark 7 until risen and golden brown.

Serves four.

HAM AND STEAK ROLL

This is my mum's version and she tells me the amounts can vary slightly depending on what you've got in stock. She cooks this in an earthenware jar or 'crock' which looks rather like a long pipe but it can be cooked in a pudding basin topped with aluminium foil that has a pleat folded in it. It's basically a meat loaf which can be eaten hot with green vegetables and potatoes or cold with salad or in sandwiches.

350 g/¾ lb rump steak
100 g/¼ lb Ayrshire bacon (middle)
1 egg
Breadcrumbs made from 1 to 2
   slices plain bread
Worcestershire sauce (optional)
Black pepper

Mince together the steak and ham. You can ask your butcher to do this if you do not have a mincer, or you can chop in a food processor. Mix with the egg and breadcrumbs and add a couple of dashes of Worcestershire sauce (if you like it) and some ground black pepper. Place in an earthenware jar or pudding basin and cover with greaseproof paper or foil that is folded into a pleat in the middle to allow the air in the jar to expand but not escape, and tie with string. Place in a large pot filled with boiling water and steam for two hours. Place a weight on top of the meat roll once it is cooked and leave overnight. This is to ensure that it is firm enough for slicing. Loosen the roll from the jar with a pallet knife.

The roll can be served hot or cold.

LORNE SAUSAGE

This is alleged to be a hangover cure. I can't vouch for that, but the traditional way of eating square or Lorne sausage, with a fried egg on top, in a bap would set anyone up for the day, hangover or not. They are available in most butchers and supermarkets in Scotland – though quality can vary vastly – and so making your own probably isn't strictly necessary.

But, for the stranded ex-pat with no access to a Scottish butcher, this might be the answer. The best quality lean mince is essential if you're making the sausagemeat yourself. This recipe makes quite a few so it's probably best to slice and freeze in small portions for a later date.

> 900 g/2 lb minced beef
> 900 g/2 lbs minced pork
> 1 egg, beaten
> 3 cups breadcrumbs or crushed rusk
> 2 tsp salt
> 2 tsp white pepper
> 2 tsp nutmeg
> 2 tsp powdered dried coriander
>   seed
> Water

Mix the beef and pork mince together thoroughly.

Mix in the beaten egg and add enough breadcrumbs to make a firm mixture. Lorne sausage has a high proportion of cereal in it so make sure you add enough to give it that characteristically grainy texture. Add the salt, pepper and spices and mix thoroughly. Add some water if the mixture is a little too firm. Form the sausage into a long cuboid shape. You could use a loaf tin for this or you could wrap it in cling film to help make it easier to shape. Place in the freezer for a short time but do not allow to freeze. This is simply to solidify the mixture to allow it to become easier to slice cleanly into that familiar trapezium shape. If you are freezing them once they are sliced, cut squares of greased paper cellophane and place between each sausage slice, to help make them easier to separate, and place a few in each freezer bag.

Fry each sausage until golden brown and crusty on each side and serve in a warm, buttered bap (see page 14) with fried onions or chutney (see page 181).

MUTTON PIE

This tasty savoury pie is a great way to use up leftovers from a roast. Alternatively, a cheap cut of meat can be stewed slowly and used as the filling.

100 g/4 oz suet
water
450 g/1 lb plain flour
Additional lukewarm water

100 g/4 oz chopped mutton or
    lamb (already roasted or stewed)
50 g/2 oz chopped mushrooms
50 g/2 oz chopped, cooked ham
grated nutmeg
salt and pepper

Preheat the oven to 220°C/425 g/gas mark 7. Melt the suet in enough boiling water to cover the bottom of a medium-sized saucepan. Sieve the flour into a mixing bowl and gradually add the melted suet and water mixture, plus enough additional lukewarm water to make a firm dough.

When cool, roll out the dough to a thickness of around 5 mm/$^{1}/_{10}$ inch, divide the pastry into two tops and two bottoms in order to make into two individual pies using pie tins or dishes.

If the meat is raw, rather than leftover, stew or slow cook it till tender it before putting it into the pie. Chop all the other ingredients and combine with the lamb.

Line the bottom of each pie tin with pastry and pour in the filling. Wet the rim of the pastry. Top the pies and crimp the layers of pastry together and make a small slit in the top of each one. Bake in the middle of the oven for around 20 to 30 minutes until the pastry is golden brown.

Serve hot with green vegetables and new potatoes. Makes two pies.

POTTED HOUGH

Before freezers and refrigerators became ubiquitous, potting was a traditional way of preserving meat and fish. Potted hough is easy and cheap to make and is delicious with freshly-made bread, spread with butter.

As with many traditional Scottish meat dishes, your local butcher is a much better bet for the ingredients of this recipe than the average supermarket.

> 450-g/1-lb hough of beef (the shin,
>   ask your butcher)
> 900-g/2-lb beef shin bone or
>   knuckle of veal
> 1 tsp salt
> ½ tsp allspice berries
> ½ tsp mace blade
> ½ tsp peppercorns
> 1 bay leaf
> Salt
> Pepper

Place the meat in a large thick-bottomed pan, and pour in enough cold water to just cover it (approximately 1.5 litres/3 pints). Tie the spices in a piece of muslin and add this to the pan. Bring to the boil and then reduce the heat and simmer for three to four hours. The meat should be very tender by now.

Drain the stock from the pan but do not throw it away. Flake the meat from the bone and shred or chop it finely. Place the stock and meat back in the pan and taste to see if you need to add additional salt and pepper. Boil again for another 10 minutes or so to ensure there is not too much liquid. Pour the mixture into small moulds or bowls and leave to cool completely.

Chill in the fridge and then serve with bread and butter or oatcakes.

SCOTCH EGGS

These eggs are great as party or picnic food and are convenient to eat on the move. They are very easy to make and can be eaten hot or cold.

> 450 g/1 lb pork or beef sausage
>   meat
> 5 hard-boiled eggs
> 1 raw egg
> 75 g/3 oz breadcrumbs, toasted
> Seasoning: pepper, salt, nutmeg
> Flour

Dust the hard-boiled eggs in flour. Mix the seasoning in with the sausage meat and divide it into five. Flatten one portion slightly and then wrap around a hard-boiled egg. Beat the raw egg and roll the meat-covered boiled egg in this mixture. then roll in the toasted breadcrumbs. Deep fry in hot oil for around 5 minutes or until you are sure that the sausage meat is cooked. Repeat this process for the other four eggs.

Allow the cooked eggs to drain on kitchen roll. Eat hot or cold. Sliced with salad is particularly nice.

Makes five.

SCOTCH PIES

One of the many places you're still likely to see this Scottish favourite is on a Saturday afternoon at the football, with mushy peas, beans or even mashed potato filling the handy lip on the top, eaten with a cup of bovril. Frankly, you can keep the hot bovril (best on buttered toast in my view), but a good Scotch pie is fast food at its tastiest. They're rarely referred to as 'Scotch' in Scotland, only ever in recipe books.

Bought Scotch pies vary greatly in quality. You can make sure that the ones that you make are good by buying quality lean minced beef (or lamb).

Hot water pastry:
225 g/8 oz lard or dripping
700 g/1½ lb self-raising flour
1 tsp salt
300 ml/10 fl oz water
Milk for glazing

Filling:
500 g/1 lb finely minced beef or
    lamb
225 g/8 oz finely crushed rusks or
    fine breadcrumbs
Seasoning of salt, white pepper, and
    mace or nutmeg

In a saucepan, melt the lard in the boiling water. Sieve the flour into a bowl that has been warmed (so that your hot fat and water mixture is not chilled by the flour). Make a well in the middle of the flour and mix in the hot fat and water mixture with a wooden spoon. Sometimes I find it easier to mix dough using the handle rather than the bowl of the spoon. Once the mixture has cooled a little, knead the dough using your hands. When the dough is smooth and elastic, leave it in a warm place until it becomes firmer yet still elastic enough to roll out. You could use glasses or jars that are around 9 to 10 cm (3$^1/_2$ to 4 inches) in diameter to shape your pie cases on if you don't have pie moulds or a deep muffin tin.

Roll out the dough till it is about 3 or 4 mm/$^1/_8$ inch thick. Cut out rounds that will fit whichever moulds you are using – the pastry should make around 15 pies or more. Cut out enough circles from the pastry to make tops for the pies.

Mix the mince with the rusk or breadcrumbs. Add water or gravy and bind together, then add the seasoning and mix thoroughly. Fill the pie shells three quarters full, add the tops and seal. Make slits, or little circles, in the pie tops to allow the steam to escape and brush with milk to glaze. Preheat the oven to 190°C/375°F/gas mark 5.

Bake for 25 minutes or until golden brown in colour. Serve hot with beans or marrowfat peas.

STEAK PIE

For most Scots, steak pie means New Year, and most of us will have it at some point over that period either as a precursor to the hangover or as the cure. It can be served with marrowfat peas in vinegar, or, for the more sophisticated, with green beans, cabbage and mashed potatoes. Some like to include sausages in the pie, and if so, it is best to grill them first before adding them to the stew. New Year is not a time for making pastry, so ready-rolled is absolutely ideal. It is also preferable to prepare the beef stew for your steak pie the day before. Second-day stew always tastes better, and it leaves you time to enjoy the Hogmanay festivities. Come dinner time on Ne'erday (New Year's Day), you just need to pop the ready-made pastry on top.

900g/2lb stewing steak
1 tbsp seasoned plain flour
50g/2oz dripping
1 large onion, chopped
3 large carrots
600m/1 pint beef stock
Couple of dashes of Worcestershire
   sauce
250 g/9 oz packet of frozen or fresh
   puff pastry

Make the stew the day before you intend to serve the pie. Toss the steak in the seasoned flour. Melt the dripping in a large saucepan and brown the meat, a little at a time, and them remove and put aside. Fry the onions and the carrots until softened slightly and then return the meat to the pan. Mix the beef stock with a couple of dashes of Worcestershire sauce (taste and add more if you like), lots of black pepper and some salt, and pour into the pan. Cover the pan and bring to the boil, after which you reduce the heat and simmer, still covered, for approximately two hours, checking occasionally. After one hour, taste the gravy and season to taste. When cooked, put aside to cool, refrigerate, and use in your steak pie the following day.

Preheat the oven to 220°C/425°F/gas mark 7. Pour the stew into a 1.5-litre/3-pint ashet (pie dish). Roll out the pastry and press down firmly around the sides of the ashet and on top of the stew. A big crust is fine here. Brush the top with beaten egg or some milk and score into criss-crosses. Make a hole in the centre to allow steam to escape. Cook for around 30 minutes in the centre of the oven and keep watch in case the pastry burns.

Serve immediately with marrowfat peas in vinegar (see pages 36 to 37) and mashed potatoes.

STOVIES

Lamb is my favourite ingredient for including in stovies, but it could be made with beef, pork or even fish. Stovies gets its name from the potatoes being cooked slowly in dripping on the stove. The high fat content and sweet flavour of the lamb goes perfectly with potatoes and is a delicious complement to the carrots and turnip, if you choose to include them as my mum always does. You'll find numerous different versions of stovies in different books, and nobody cooks it quite the same way. Truth is, it probably doesn't matter. As long as you have quality ingredients you can't really fail. Stovies is perfect for using up leftovers from a roast, but fresh chopped or minced meat works equally well.

2 tbsps dripping
650 g/1½ lb potatoes, sliced
1 onion, chopped
2 carrots, sliced (optional)
½ a small turnip (optional)
2 tbsps stock or meat jelly
100 g/4 oz lamb, cooked
Salt and pepper
Lamb stock

Melt the dripping in a large pan and cook the

chopped onion in it until softened and almost brown. Add the chopped potatoes and mix thoroughly with the onions and dripping. Add the chopped carrots and turnip, if you are using them, and mix through. Heat the stock or meat jelly and pour over the vegetables. Add the chopped, cooked lamb and mix with the vegetables. Season with salt and pepper. Cover the pot and cook over a low heat for around 30 minutes or until the potatoes are soft and floury. Keep a jug of stock nearby, and if you suspect the mixture is starting to burn, or stick to the pan, or is just getting too dry, then add more stock. Actually, I quite like stovies which has started to get a bit too brown on the bottom or has 'caught' as my mum calls it. Like soup, stovies is often much tastier the day after it has been cooked.

Serves four people.

HAGGIS

It would be dishonest not to admit that it is far, far easier to buy good quality haggis from any supermarket (MacSween's is deserving in its reputation as the best) than to prepare it from the traditional recipe of boiling of a sheep's pluck (stomach) and lights (lungs, heart and liver). It would also be dishonest to claim that the purchase of a sheep's pluck in this day and age would be easy. But what book on Scottish cookery would be complete without the traditional recipe for our national dish? Some people who have never tasted haggis view it with a trepidation normally reserved for the cuisine of Mongolian nomads.

Don't let the rather medieval preparation of the ingredients scare you, because this spicy, delicious, aromatic sausage is worthy of its title as 'Great Chieftain o' the puddin' race'. Most countries have a sausage dish such as this but haggis's fame as a Scottish delicacy, and indeed as our national dish, probably lies primarily with the popularity of the life and works of Robert Burns and his poem 'Address to a Haggis'. On January 25, Burns suppers are held all over the world, not just by ex-pats, and no Burns supper would be acceptable without one.

The following recipe is adapted from Mistress Margaret Dods' Cook and Housewife Manual, first published 1826. Meg or Margaret Dods was the pseudonym of Christian Isobel Johnstone (1781–1857) a writer and editor. The book was at first dismissed as a literary joke because Johnstone took her nom de plume from the fictional landlady of the Cleikum Inn in Sir Walter Scott's novel St Ronan's Well, *but a revised edition of 1829 became considered as a useful household manual.*

The best way of judging the seasoning is to add seasoning to the meat mixture gradually, take pinches of the mixture and frying in a pan, tasting until you find it satisfactory.

> The pluck (stomach) and lights
>   (heart, liver and lungs) of a sheep
> 4 or 5 onions
> 2 cups finely ground oatmeal,
>   toasted
> 450g/1 lb beef suet
> Pepper
> Salt
> Cayenne pepper
> Beef gravy
> The juice of a lemon

Wash the stomach thoroughly and turn it inside out. Pour boiling water over it and scrape with a knife. It is best to soak the stomach in salted water overnight.

After washing the heart, liver and lungs, pierce the heart and liver to let any blood flow out and parboil the whole (the heart, liver and lungs should still be attached to one another), leaving the windpipe hanging out of the pot. After a few minutes, change the water in the pot for fresh. Let the pluck boil for a further half hour and then remove from the pot. Cut the liver in half and return half to the pot. Remove any gristle. Chop the lungs, heart and half liver extremely finely (most easily done these days in a food processor). Blend the meat with the 2 cups of toasted oatmeal, the onions and a pound of beef suet. Grate or process the other half of the liver and mix with the other ingredients.

Season the meat and prepare to stuff the stomach bag. Place the meat in the bag and pour in the beef gravy, being careful not to fill the bag too full or it may burst. Allow room for the oatmeal to swell. Add the juice of one lemon and tie up the bag securely, taking care not to trap too much air. (This recipe is for a very large haggis. It might be better to split this mixture into two or three haggises [haggi?]).

The liquid in which the pluck was boiled is the ideal liquor in which to cook the haggis. Place the haggis in a large pan containing the strained liquid, and boil. Prick the bag when it begins to swell and boil for a further three hours.

EASY HAGGIS

An easy way of making haggis at home can be found in this recipe. There's not a sheep's stomach in sight – just some aluminium foil and a pudding basin. If sheep's liver cannot be obtained try calf's or pig's.

> 200 g/8 oz sheep's liver
> 100 g/4 oz beef suet
> 2 large onions
> 100 g/4 oz toasted oatmeal
> salt and white pepper

Boil the liver in a pan filled with water for around 40 minutes. Retain this water once the liver is cooked and remove the liver from the pan. Mince the liver finely. Cook the onions on a low heat in a frying pan with a little of the suet. Don't brown the onions, but cook then till they are soft. Chop them finely with the rest of the suet. Toast the oatmeal in a frying pan. Combine all the ingredients in a bowl and season with the salt and pepper. Fine black pepper powder will give a more authentic taste than freshly ground black pepper.

Moisten the mixture using the liquid in which the liver was cooked. Press the mixture lightly into a pudding basin, cover the top with aluminium foil, pleated once to allow expansion and tied in

place, and place in a large pot, one third full of water, and boil for 2 hours.

Serve with mashed potato and mashed turnip and butter, or with clapshot (see page 65).

MEAT AND GAME

MARGARET HAMMOND'S POT ROAST PHEASANT WITH ELDERBERRY SAUCE

Pheasant can be quite a dry meat so this method of slow cooking on the stove is a great one for ensuring that the bird is always surrounded by juices. And a good sauce is also essential. This recipe was my Aunt Margaret's, who was a great cook and also a dab hand with home-made wine, hence the elderberry sauce. Since the pheasants she used were generally unplucked when she got them she found that it was easier to skin the bird and cook in a pot rather than pluck and roast. However, some fat (which keeps the bird moist and tasty) will be lost using this method so ensure the bird is seared and well basted with butter. If the bird is older and possibly tougher then this slow cooking is also a good method of cooking.

Generally you would roast a pheasant, with its skin 'barded' with fatty bacon, in the oven at 230ºC/450ºF/gas mark 8 for 8 to 10 minutes, then at 200ºC/400ºF/gas mark 6 for 30 to 50 minutes or until brown.

One average-sized pheasant will feed two to three people. Pheasants are in season between October 1 and February 1 (shooting season). It is traditional to serve a 'brace' of pheasants, that is, one male and one female, and although the male is the more flamboyant-looking of the two, the dull plumage of the female belies a better flavour. Game birds are best eaten young and the best guide to recognising this is the plumage. Young birds have softer, more even feathers than older birds. Pheasant should be hung for between 3 to 10 days, so be sure to check with your butcher to see if it has been hung and for how long.

1 pheasant, plucked or skin removed
Butter
Stock or water

For the sauce:
1 large onion, finely chopped
100 g/½ lb unsalted butter
280 ml/10 fl oz carton of double
    cream
Pepper
Elderberry wine (use a fruity, heavy
    red wine like a shiraz/syrah if you
    can't get elderberry)

In a well-buttered, heavy-bottomed casserole pot, place a pheasant, also well-buttered. Sear the bird all over in the pot. Add a cup of water or stock to the pan, cover the pheasant in more butter and cover. Simmer over a moderate heat for 30 to 40 minutes and keep basting the bird in the juices.

Once cooked, remove the bird from the pot and

place on a carving plate.

To the cooking pot add the onion and cook in the juices and additional butter over a low heat till soft, for approximately 5 minutes. Do not allow the onion to colour, but cook till soft and sweet. Season with black pepper and pour in a generous glass of elderberry wine. Reduce until there is almost no liquid left and then add the cream. Boil for around 5 minutes and then force through a sieve with a wooden spoon (alternatively, blend using a hand blender).

Serve the bird with roast potatoes or game chips (thinly sliced fried potatoes, see pages 105 to 106), parsnips and carrots.

ROAST GROUSE WITH GAME CHIPS

Grouse is best bought in early September at the middle of the season, which is from August 12 to December 10. Grouse should be hung for between three to ten days. Grouse are small birds so they don't need to be roasted long, and they should be barded with fatty bacon and basted regularly to help keep them moist while roasting.

2 young grouse
25 g/2 oz butter
Lemon juice
4 rashers streaky bacon
More butter for basting

Game chips:
450 g/1 lb potatoes, sliced
   lengthways, very thinly
Beef dripping

Preheat the oven to 200ºC/400ºF/gas mark 6. Mix a squeeze of lemon juice with the butter, smear a little over the skins of each bird and then a place some inside each bird. Wrap the bacon over the birds and place in a roasting tin in the middle of the oven.

For the game chips, while the birds are cooking, melt some dripping and coat your thinly-sliced potatoes. Spread them out evenly on a baking tray and roast until golden brown and crispy. Drain on kitchen roll and then keep warm. Alternatively you can deep-fry them.

You should cook the grouse for around 30 minutes and baste them regularly. Just before they are cooked you could dust them lightly with a little flour and return them to the oven to brown. When cooked, the flesh of the birds should still be slightly pink near the bone.

Serve with the warm game chips and skirlie (see page 71).

ROAST LEG OF SCOTCH LAMB

You don't need to mess about too much with good quality meat and this recipe is about as simple as it gets. Lamb and rosemary were made for each other and while perhaps some would suggest that you should probably accompany it with a vegetable of a contrasting flavour, roast potatoes and rosemary are perfect too. The smell as it cooks is almost better than the finished dish – almost!

1 2.2-kg/5-lb leg of lamb
Butter
Sea salt
6 sprigs of fresh rosemary
Lamb stock
Balsamic vinegar
Red wine

6 large floury potatoes
4 large parnips (really, just as many as you think you will all eat)

Rub the meat all over a with a generous quantity of butter and place on a roasting pan. Sprinkle with a little sea salt. Chop half of the rosemary roughly and sprinkle over the butter-covered joint, then snap the remainder into little sprigs that can be shoved into the flesh of the lamb. Roast for twenty minutes in an oven preheated to 220ºC/425ºF/gas mark 7. While the lamb is roasting, prepare the roast potatoes and parsnips. Cut the potatoes into quarters, and the parsnips lengthways into fingers, and parboil for around 10 to 15 minutes. Baste in oil and cover in ground sea salt and chopped rosemary and roast till they are golden brown.

Reduce the heat to 190ºC/375ºF/gas mark 5 and roast for a further hour. Remove the lamb from the roasting pan and leave it to rest for around 20 to 30 minutes. Move the pan to the top of the stove in order to make a gravy. Turn on a low heat and heat the pan. Add a generous splash of good balsamic vinegar to the pan and mix with the lamb juices with a wooden spoon. Add about half a glass of red wine and reduce. Taste the gravy and season as necessary.

Serve with the roast vegetables and boiled peas.
Serves four to six (with leftovers).

JUGGED HARE WITH FORCEMEAT BALLS

In the days before Pyrex they would have used a jug for cooking the hare in, or else a tall covered earthenware pot like the 'crock' I mentioned in the recipe for ham and steak roll. These days, a large casserole with a lid is easier to find though ovenproof jugs are still available for this purpose.

The hare:
1 hare, cut into egg-sized joints
75 g/3 oz butter
500 ml/1 pint stock (vegetable or chicken)
1 wineglass port
2 finely chopped onions
1 stick celery
Juice of half a lemon
2.5 cm/1-inch cinnamon stick
4 cloves
1 bay leaf
Salt
6 peppercorns, crushed

Gravy:
The blood drained from the hare
2 level tsps arrowroot
Salt and pepper

Forcemeat balls:
The liver from the hare
100 g/4 oz streaky bacon
75 g/3 oz shredded suet
150 g/6 oz white breadcrumbs
1 tbsp chopped fresh parsley
1 pinch dried thyme
1 pinch nutmeg
2 egg yolks

Soak the pieces of hare in cold, salted water overnight. Drain off the water and dry the pieces. Melt the butter in a large frying pan and fry the joints briskly to brown them evenly. As they are fried, pack them into the cooking dish (a 2.5-litre/5-pint casserole dish).

Add the finely chopped onions, chopped celery and a generous sprinkling of salt and crushed peppercorns. Pour the stock over the meat and then follow this with the glass of port. Add the lemon juice, cinnamon stick, cloves and bay leaf and place the lid on the dish. Cook the hare in an oven at 150°C/300°F/gas mark 2 for between two and three hours or until the meat is tender.

Make the forcemeat balls while the hare is cooking. Mince the bacon with the hare's liver and then combine this with the breadcrumbs, suet, parsley, thyme and nutmeg. Bind this together with the beaten egg yolks. Season well with salt and pepper. Make into small balls around the size of a walnut and fry in a pan by rolling them around till they are brown all over

When the hare is ready, pour the gravy from the casserole dish into a saucepan. Blend the arrowroot with a little water and them add to the blood from the hare. Stir this into the gravy and bring very slowly to the boil, then simmer till thickened. Taste and season with salt and pepper if necessary. A spoonful of redcurrant jelly is nice to include in the sauce if you have it. Pour the gravy around the joints of hare. Serve the hare and forcemeat balls together with the gravy and some more redcurrant jelly.

Serve with roast vegetables and game chips (see pages 105 to 106).

DESSERTS

ATHOLL BROSE

Traditionally, Atholl Brose was a drink made from oatmeal bree (the liquid strained from a mixture of oatmeal and water that has been left to stand for an hour and is then strained through a sieve), honey and whisky.

I have never tried the drink but I can't say I really find the idea appealing, and a lot of people share my reluctance. This variation however is a pudding derived from the same ingredients but with the addition of whipped double cream. To garnish, fresh Scottish raspberries or blackberries are delicious.

100g/4 oz toasted coarse or
medium oatmeal, reserve a
little for garnish if you like
2 tbsps heather honey
125 ml/¼ pint whisky
250 ml/½ pint double cream

Preheat the oven to 200ºC/400ºF/gas mark 6. Spread the oatmeal evenly over the bottom of a baking tray and toast in the centre of the oven, shaking the tin occasionally, for about 15 minutes, until the oats are a deep golden brown.

Add the honey and the whisky to 90 g/3¹/₂ oz of the oats. Whip the cream until it reaches a firm consistency and fold in the oats mixture.

Serve immediately in tall stemmed glasses with a light sprinkling of the remaining oats.

BREAD AND BUTTER PUDDING

This is a pudding that has, in recent years, experienced renewed popularity. It is cheap and easy to make and can make use of leftover bread that has become too dry to eat on its own.

600 ml/1 pt single cream
25 g/1 oz caster sugar
Yolks of 4 large eggs
1 tsp vanilla extract
8 slices of buttered bread
50 g/2 oz sultanas
Muscovado sugar
Single cream for pouring

Heat the milk in a saucepan until it is beginning to bubble, but not boil. Beat together the sugar and the egg yolks in a large bowl and then gradually whisk the hot milk into this mixture with a balloon whisk. Add the vanilla extract. Once the eggs and milk are thoroughly whisked pour the mixture back into the saucepan, and cook for around 8 minutes over a gentle heat, still never allowing to boil. Butter the 8 slices of bread and cut in halves diagonally. Place in an oven-proof dish, pointed corners upwards, and scatter the sultanas throughout. Pour the custard over the bread and make sure that every piece of bread is thoroughly soaked in the mixture. Sprinkle muscovado sugar over the top and place in a pre-heated oven at 180°C/350°F/gas mark 4 for about 30 or 40 minutes or until the custard has set and the top is golden brown and crispy.

Serve hot with single cream.

BURNT CREAM

Burnt Cream, or Crème Brulée, is famously associated with Trinity College Cambridge but can be traced to nineteenth-century Scotland. It's a very rich dish that should be flavoured with vanilla extract rather that vanilla essence. It's nice to see the seeds from vanilla pods in the custard. Slit a vanilla pod lengthways, scrape out the seeds and add them to the cream. Drop the vanilla pod into the cream too but remove when the custard starts to thicken.

> 500 ml/1 pint double cream
> 4 egg yolks
> 3 level tbsps caster sugar
> 2 drops vanilla extract, or one
>   vanilla pod halved, with seeds
>   scraped off and added to the pan
> Caster or brown sugar for the top of
>   the custard

Preheat the oven to 180°C/350°F/gas mark 4.

Add the cream, and vanilla pod if you're using it, to a saucepan and very slowly bring to just below boiling point. Beat the eggs yolks together with the 3 tbsps caster sugar in a large bowl. To this bowl you gradually beat in the almost boiling cream (not the other way round) and then, when thoroughly beaten together, return the mixture to the saucepan. Cook on a low heat, taking care not to boil it, for around 5 to 10 minutes, stirring continuously. Add the vanilla extract if you're using it, or remove the vanilla pod at this stage if that was your choice to flavour the custard.

Pour the custard into an ovenproof dish. Fill a roasting tray half full with boiling water. I find it is easiest and safest to open the oven that has been preheating, pull out a shelf in the middle, place the roasting pan on the shelf and pour in the boiling water from the kettle as it sits on the shelf. Then place the dish in the hot water on the tray. Cook the custard until it has lightly set which should be around 40 minutes, but check the consistency by tapping it with a spoon or a finger.

Leave this to cool and then chill in the refrigerator overnight. The next day sprinkle with caster or brown sugar and caramelise either using a chef's blow torch or under the grill. Chill again so that the caramelised sugar is crunchy.

Serve with Scottish raspberries. This dish can also be made in individual ramekin dishes but you must reduce the cooking time a little.

CLOUTIE DUMPLING

You'll need to have a whole morning free, and a considerable part of the afternoon, in order to do justice to this spicy and delicious dumpling.

125 g/4 oz suet, chopped
250 g/8 oz self-raising flour
1 tsp baking powder
125 g/4 oz breadcrumbs
75 g/3 oz brown sugar
1 grated apple
200 g/8 oz currants and sultanas
1 tsp each cinnamon, ginger, nutmeg
1 tbsp golden (or maple) syrup
2 eggs
About 1 cup of milk

Half fill a very large pot and bring to the boil. Scald a large piece of linen or cheesecloth with boiling water then dust it with flour. Beat the eggs, mix in the syrup and a little milk, and gradually mix into the dry ingredients and fruit.

Place the mixture in the middle of the cloth. Tie securely but allow for swelling. Place an inverted plate on the bottom of the pan and put the pudding on it. Boil for 3 to 4 hours. Never allow the water to drop below half the depth of the pudding. Dip in cold water, remove the cloth and dry the pudding off in a medium-to-hot oven. Sprinkle the top with sugar and serve with cream or custard.

SMIDDY DUMPLING

This recipe is a very old east coast variation of dumpling which was given to my Aunt Jean Thomson around 70 years ago. The origin of the name has never been known in our family but it was being cooked like this long before Aunt Jean fell heir to the recipe. Jean was still cooking it well into her nineties. This method is a lot less time comsuming than the traditional one but just as delicious.

1 cup sugar
¾ cup sultanas
4 oz/100 g butter
1 cup water
1 tsp baking soda
1 tsp mixed spice

Bring all of the above ingredients to the boil in a large heavy bottomed pot for around two minutes. When this mixture is cool add:

1 cup plain flour
1 cup self raising flour
2 eggs, beaten

Combine all the ingredients well and place in a large, buttered, round cake tin. Cook for 1½ hours at 150ºC/300ºF.

CRANACHAN

There are lots of variations on this recipe but the basic staple of it remains the same, usually: cream, sometimes Scottish curd cheese called crowdie, honey, oats, and whisky or Drambuie. The ingredients would often have been put out individually in bowls and the diners would have helped themselves and made their own combinations.

Many cooks like to fold Scottish raspberries into the mixture. The tartness of the raspberries cuts through the creaminess. Just take care not to reduce the rasperries to mush – fold them in gently

It's possible to cheat when it comes to the oats. Rather than toasting rolled oats, you can sneakily include honey- or sugar-coated toasted oatmeal breakfast cereal (without raisins of course), placed in a plastic bag and lightly crushed with a rolling pin.

If you would would rather do things properly and sugar-coat the oats yourself, sprinkle some rolled oats on a baking tray and top with a handful of brown sugar, or drizzle with honey. Place on the top shelf of a hot oven till the sugar has melted and covers the oats. Take great care that this does not burn or it will be unusable.

1 or 2 tbsps Drambuie or whisky
250 ml/½ pint double cream,
   whipped
100 g/4 oz of honey-toasted
   oatmeal
250 g/9 oz raspberries
Heather honey

Whip the cream with the alcohol until thick but not too firm. Fold in the honeyed oats. Carefully fold in the raspberries, taking care not to break them up too much.

Serve in glasses topped with a little more honeyed oats and a drizzle of heather honey. Pour over a little more whisky or Drambuie at this stage if you want but don't allow it to become runny.

Serves four.

GROSERT FOOL

Grosert is Scots for gooseberry. This is a variation on the traditional grosert fool which would have entailed cooking and sieving the fruit first before whipping with the cream, after which, the dish could have been frozen like an ice cream. This recipe makes use of produce that is already frozen, which is particularly handy for those of us who grow our own fruit and stash the surplus in the freezer at the end of the season, or if you have bought frozen gooseberries out of season. This recipe works equally well with other berries and soft fruit.

450 g/1 lb gooseberries, frozen
100–150 g/4–6 oz sugar
½ pint double cream

Allow the gooseberries to half-defrost. When they are just becoming soft enough to liquidise, but are still partially crystallised, blend them in a food processor or liquidiser with the sugar and the cream. Blend till the fruit is in quite small pieces and cream has become lightly whipped. Return to the freezer for a short period to make extra chilled, but don't totally freeze, and then serve immediately in tall-stemmed glasses.

Serves four.

SCOTCH TRIFLE

This is also known as Typsy Laird for the reason that it has a generous splash of Drambuie as its defining ingredient. Everyone has their own variation on what should go in a trifle and so it seems rather gratuitous to include measurements, because it's mostly judged by eye and personal taste. So feel free to take liberties with the ingredients listed below.

It's also very nice to make individual trifles, especially if you're entertaining as it all looks a bit neater and you don't get left with a soup of mixed up trifle at the bottom of the bowl. However, although this soupy bit might not look too attractive, it still tastes fabulous.

Custard:
600 ml/1 pt single cream
25 g/1 oz caster sugar
Yolks of 4 large eggs
1 tsp vanilla extract

The trifle:
6 sponge cakes (or enough sponge
    to cover the bottom of the dish
    you are going to use)
Raspberry jam
150 g/5 oz Rataffia or Amaretti
    biscuits

6 tbsps (or a generous splash) of
   Drambuie (enough to moisten the
   sponges)
2 (supermarket size) punnets of
   raspberries
300 ml/10 fl oz double cream,
   whipped
Flaked almonds for topping

To make the custard, heat the milk in a saucepan until it is beginning to bubble, but not boil. Beat together the sugar and the egg yolks in a large bowl and to this egg mixture gradually whisk in the hot milk with a balloon whisk. It's easier to combine them this way, rather than the other way round, and this way you'll not lose any of the egg mixture. Add the vanilla extract. Once the eggs and milk are thoroughly whisked pour the mixture back into the saucepan, over a gentle heat, and cook for around 8 minutes, still never allowing to boil. Leave the custard to cool while you prepare the other ingredients.

Spread the sponges generously with raspberry jam and place in the bottom of your trifle bowl which should be glass or crystal so that you can see the layers. Break up the ratafia biscuits a little and sprinkle over the top of the sponges. On top of this, drizzle the Drambuie. Five or six tablespoons should be enough to moisten it and you don't want the bottom of the trifle to become too sloppy.

On top of this layer spread the raspberries. If the custard is sufficiently cooled then pour it over the raspberries and chill in the fridge until you are ready to serve. Just before serving, spread with whipped cream and cover with flaked almonds.

Makes around six servings.

STEAMED PUDDING WITH DRAMBUIE SYRUP

Steamed puddings are experiencing a renaissance in restaurants after years of being persona, or pudding, non grata. Their stodgy comfort-food status is now their virtue. This scullery classic, usually served with golden syrup, is here made with a rich and alcoholic Drambuie syrup.

100 g/4 oz butter
100 g/4 oz caster sugar
2 large eggs
175 g/6 oz self-raising flour
2 tbsps milk

8 tbsps of golden syrup
6 tbsps Drambuie

You will need a 1-litre/1³⁄₄-pint pudding basin which has been thoroughly buttered. Mix the Drambuie and the syrup together in a saucepan and boil to reduce the liquid slightly. Allow to cool slightly and then pour half of the syrup into the buttered pudding basin. Chill in the fridge for an hour so that the syrup is very thick.

Cream the butter and sugar together, then gradually fold in the flour and egg to the mixture in alternate spoonfuls. Once the mixture is smooth and totally combined, pour into the pudding basin that has been chilling in the fridge. Place tin foil that has been pleated, to allow expansion, over the top of the basin and tie with string. Don't allow too much of the foil to be folded over the edge of the basin and don't let it sit in the water.

Place the basin in a large pot. Around it, carefully pour boiling water to reach half way up the basin. Simmer, rather than boil, with the pot covered, for around two hours. Watch the level of the water and top up if needed. Test the pudding by piercing it with a long metal skewer. If the skewer comes out clean, the pudding is ready.

Remove from the pan and leave the pudding to rest in the basin for around five minutes. Run a flexible, round-tipped knife around the edge of the basin, place a large warmed plate on the top and then carefully turn it upside down.

Serve sliced with Drambuie syrup poured around and with single cream or custard.

CAKES, BISCUITS AND TEA BREADS

ABERNETHY BISCUITS

The recipe for these buttery treats sometimes includes a teaspoon of caraway seeds. This addition is, it is said, how the biscuits got their name as their inclusion was suggested by a Dr John Abernethy.

>250 g/8 oz flour
>1 level tsp cream of tartar
>¾ level tsp baking soda
>75 g/3 oz butter
>25 g/1 oz lard
>75 g/3 oz sugar
>1 tbsp milk
>1 egg, beaten
>Pinch of salt

Sieve the flour and the raising agents. Cut the fat into cubes and sprinkle into the flour. With cold hands (run them under the cold tap if they are too warm) and with a light touch rub the fat into the flour until it reaches a breadcrumb consistency. Add the sugar and mix until evenly distributed. Add the milk and enough beaten egg to form into a stiff dough. Roll till about 6 mm/¼ inch thick and cut into biscuits. Prick the surface of the biscuits with a fork and bake at 190ºC/375ºF/gas mark 5 for around 15 minutes or until golden brown.

DATE AND WALNUT LOAF

This loaf is a moist and aromatic treat for afternoon tea. This recipe is for a large loaf but the mixture can be divided into two smaller tins and baked for a shorter time.

    1 cup boiling water
    250 g/8 oz stoned dates
    2 level tsps bicarbonate of soda
    1 pinch of salt
    125 g/4 oz sugar
    125 g/4 oz butter
    1 egg
    425 g/14 oz plain flour
    50 g/2 oz chopped walnuts
    1 tsp vanilla extract

Set the oven to 180°C/350°F/gas mark 4. Pour the boiling water over the dates and add the bicarbonate of soda. Leave this to stand while you cream together the butter and sugar. Whisk the eggs. Then sieve the flour and add the salt to it. Fold in alternate spoonfuls of beaten egg and flour into the creamed butter and sugar until smooth. Mix the dates and the water in with the mixture and add the vanilla. Grease a 20-cm/8-inch loaf tin. Pour the mixture into the tin and then place on the middle shelf of the oven for an hour. When cooled slice and spread with butter.

DUNDEE CAKE

Along with jute, jam and journalism Dundee is also famous for cake. Dundee also produced marmalade and that is why this cake uses fresh orange peel.

300 g/11 oz plain flour
15 g/½ oz self-raising flour
200 g/8 oz butter
200 g/8 oz brown sugar
25 g/1 oz ground almonds
6 eggs
200 g/8 oz orange peel, chopped
700 g/26 oz sultanas
2 tsps black treacle
1 tbsp of brandy or whisky

Sieve the flour together. Cream together the butter and brown sugar. Whisk the eggs together. Add a spoonful of flour to the creamed butter and sugar and mix together either with a wooden spoon or with a cake mixer. Then add a spoonful of the beaten egg. Add alternate spoonfuls of egg and flour until they are all mixed together. Take care not to add too much egg at at time or the mixture may curdle. If this happens add more flour and beat the mixture strongly. Add the fruit and the alcohol. Pour into a greased, 18-cm/7-inch cake tin and place the halves of almonds on the top. Bake for approximately 2 to 2¼ hours at 180ºC/350ºF/gas mark 4, in the centre of the oven.

FRUIT GIRDLE SCONES

These scones will be slightly flatter and less raised than those cooked in the oven. If you don't have a girdle then a heavy-bottomed frying pan will be fine.

250 g/8 oz self raising flour
100 g/4 oz butter
¼ tsp salt
¼ tsp mixed spice
1 cup milk or buttermilk
50 g/2 oz currants

Rub the fat into the sieved flour to make a breadcrumb consistency. Add the currants and spice and mix thoroughly. Gradually mix in enough milk to make a soft elastic dough. Gently roll out the dough on a floured surface to about 2 cm/³/₄ inch in thickness. Cut into rounds with a cutter. Heat a griddle, or a heavy-bottomed pan, to a medium heat. To test the heat of the girdle sprinkle a little flour on it and if it colours slightly in a few seconds it is hot enough. Cook on each side for around 4 minutes or until browned and risen. Serve hot or cold.

Makes approximately ten to twelve cakes depending on the size of the cutter.

FRUIT LOAF

You can add an ounce of mixed peel to this recipe if desired and reduce the sultanas to 100 g/4 oz.

400 g/14 oz plain flour
2 tsps baking powder
1 tsp bicarbonate of soda
100 g/4 oz butter
200 g/8 oz caster sugar
100 g/4 oz raisins
100 g/4 oz currants
125 g/5 oz sultanas
250 ml/½ pint sour milk

Use a 900-g/2-lb loaf tin. Preheat the oven to 180ºC/350ºF/gas mark 4. Sieve the flour and baking powder into a bowl, then rub in the butter with your fingers. Add the sugar and also blend this through with your fingers. Add the dried fruit and mix thoroughly. Bind the mixture together with the sour milk. Grease the loaf tin and line with baking parchment. Fill the loaf tin with the mixture and bake at 180ºC/350ºF/gas mark 4 for one hour. Reduce the heat to 160ºC/325ºF/gas mark 3 for a further hour. Test the loaf with a skewer after about 40 minutes. It is best to store the loaf in an airtight container for two days before cutting and spreading with butter.

ISA'S LOAF

This is the only name I have ever known for this lovely, moist, sconey loaf, the Isa in question being my Great Aunt Isa Brownlee. It's reminiscent of Madeira cake but I far prefer this one, especially with its crust of caster sugar on top.

It's also an easy recipe to remember because (in imperial measures at least) the measurements are 5,4,3,2,1. The five tablespoons of flour need to be generously heaped tablespoons. Choose a strong tasting, salted butter for a very buttery flavoured loaf.

5 heaped tbsps self-raising flour
4 tbsps milk
3 tbsps sugar
2 oz/50 g butter
1 egg (large)
A generous sprinkling of caster
    sugar for the top of the loaf

Sieve the flour. Mix the milk with the sugar and the beaten egg. Melt the butter. Gradually beat together, with electric beaters or a whisk, the milk and sugar mixture, the flour, and the melted butter. You should do this gradually or the mixture might curdle. If it does curdle, beat in a little (very little) more flour.

Pour into a loaf tin and sprinkle the top with caster sugar. Bake at 180°C/350°F/gas mark 4 for 30 minutes.

Cool and serve in slices spread with butter.

GINGERBREAD SQUARES

Some gingerbread recipes use treacle, but you get a milder flavour, although a lighter colour, by using golden syrup.

450 g/1 lb self-raising flour
1 tsp mixed spice
1 tsp cinnamon
1 tsp ginger
100 g/4 oz golden syrup
100 g/4 oz butter
100 g/4 oz caster sugar
2 eggs, separated
100 g/4 oz sultanas
50 g/2 oz crystallised ginger, finely
    chopped
250 ml/½ pint milk

Sieve the flour and spices together. Beat the egg yolks and sugar together. Melt the butter and syrup together and then add to the egg yolks and sugar. Mix in the dry ingredients and then gradually beat in the milk. Beat the egg whites till stiff and fold into the mixture. Add the chopped ginger and sultanas. Pour into a greased 30-cm/12-inch tin, place in the middle of the oven and cook at 180ºC/350ºF/gas mark 4, for 1 hour. Cool on a rack and then cut into squares.

OATCAKES

These oatcakes will improve every time you make them. Traditionally they would have been made with melted beef dripping. These savoury cakes are perfect with soft or hard cheese, butter, honey or jam.

> 100 g/4 oz medium oatmeal
> 100 g/4 oz coarse oatmeal
> 100 g/4 oz fine oatmeal or barley
>   meal
> 25 g/1 oz butter, melted
>   (traditionally beef dripping would
>   have been used)
> Generous pinch baking soda
> ½ tsp salt
> 4 to 7 tsps hot water

Preheat the oven to 150°C/300°F/gas mark 2. Mix the oatmeal together and mix 250g/10 oz of the mixture with the baking soda. Reserve 50 g/2 oz of the meal for when you are rolling out the mixture later on.

Melt the butter or dripping and blend the fat with the meal. To this mixture, slowly add enough hot water to make a smooth but stiff paste.

Form the dough into a ball and roll it out on a board that is sprinkled with half of the remaining

oatmeal. Flatten this ball with your hands and sprinkle it with the last of the oatmeal. Make sure all of the surface is thoroughly covered with meal and then roll out into a circle until quite thin, that is, about 0.5 cm/$\frac{1}{8}$ inch thick. Cut it into eight wedges. Carefully transfer these wedges to a greased baking sheet, a fish slice is probably best for this. Bake in the centre of the oven for around 30 minutes without allowing to become too brown.

Makes eight oatcakes.

EMPIRE BISCUITS

This recipe is my Aunt Babs's and she makes the lightest empire biscuits you'll ever taste.

> 75 g/3 oz butter or margarine
> 25 g/1 oz sugar
> 100 g/4 oz self-raising flour
> Raspberry jam or jelly
> 150 g/6 oz icing sugar
> Approx. 2 tsps water
> Lemon juice

Beat the butter and sugar together to a cream. Sieve the flour and mix it gradually into the butter and sugar until it forms a firmish dough. Roll out thinly (about 3 or 4 mm/$1/8$ inch) and cut into rounds using a pastry cutter or a drinking glass. Bake on the middle shelf of the oven for around 10 minutes 180ºC/350ºF/gas mark 4, or until golden, but not too brown.

Makes around a dozen biscuits depending on the size of your cutter. Cool and spread half of the biscuits with jam on their rough sides. Sandwich each biscuit together with another, again rough side towards the jam. Mix up the icing sugar, water and a squirt of lemon juice and coat the top of each sandwiched biscuit. Leave to set.

SCOTCH PANCAKES

Also known as drop scones, these Scotch pancakes should take about ten minutes to make and taste best eaten straight from the girdle, drizzled with golden syrup. I guarantee you won't be able to resist them. They are are also acceptably tasty cold, spread with butter and jam. Fried second-day pancakes can also make a rather indulgent addition to the already indulgent Scottish fry-up.

> 200 g/8 oz plain flour
> 1 tsp baking soda
> 2 tsps cream of tartar
> ½ tsp salt
> 25 g/1 oz sugar
> 1 large egg
> 250 ml/½ pint milk

Sieve together the flour, baking soda, cream of tartar and salt. Dissolve the sugar in the milk. Beat the egg and mix with the milk. Gradually beat together the liquid and the dry ingredients with a balloon whisk, taking care not to create any lumps. Beat until you have a smooth but relatively thick batter.

Heat a girdle or thick-bottomed frying pan and smear with a thin coating of butter.

Drop spoonfuls of the mixture onto the girdle,

around four at a time. When the surfaces of the pancakes show some bubbling, flip them over and brown the other side. Place the cooked pancakes in a clean tea towel as you cook them, and fold it over them.

SCONES

Scones are perfect for afternoon tea and taste equally good with sweet fillings such as jam and cream or savoury fillings such as cheese or meats. In fact this recipe was in my granny's recipe book as 'afternoon tea scones', as opposed to 'plain oven scones'. The difference being the inclusion of caster sugar in the former and the shape of the scone as a large round in the latter.

Scones take a bit of practice and a light hand to get right so don't be disheartened if your first attempts aren't as light and fluffy as you would prefer. Scones taste best and are at their lightest when eaten hot from the oven. Serve with butter or whipped cream and home made jam.

> 200 g/8 oz self-raising flour
> 40 g/1 ½ oz slightly salted butter, diced
> 1 tbsp caster sugar
> 1 cup of milk
> ¼ tsp salt

Sieve the flour and sugar into a large mixing bowl and drop in the cubes of butter. Rub the fat into the flour and sugar with the fingertips, lightly. Try to make sure that your hands are not too hot. Add the milk and mix to a soft dough that is elastic and not too sticky. Do not overmix or the scones will be heavy. Sieve some flour onto a work surface and turn out the dough.

Flatten to around 2 cm/1 inch thick but try not to handle the dough too much, so do this quickly. Cut into circles with a cutter and brush with a little milk or beaten egg. Sieve some flour onto a greased baking sheet and evenly space the scones on the sheet.

Don't place them too close together, allow for expansion. Bake near the top of the oven for around 15 to 20 minutes at 180°C/360°F/gas mark 4.

SELKIRK BANNOCK

Unlike Pitcaithly bannocks (page 154) and oatmeal bannocks (or oatcakes page 144) this is a teabread. Traditionally the Selkirk bannock made use of leftover bread dough, which used to be readily available from the baker. Today, since it's unlikely that you're going to have such a thing as leftover bread dough, this recipe includes instructions on making the dough. Most recipes for Selkirk bannock include mixed peel, but I have a particular aversion to it and prefer to substitute more sultanas instead.

    450 g/1 lb flour
    Pinch of salt
    1 sachet of easy-blend dried yeast
    25 g/1 oz caster sugar
    250 ml/9 fl oz warm semi-skimmed
       milk (or half
       full-cream milk, half water)
    75 g/2½ oz butter
    225g/8 oz sultanas (if you want,
       substitute 50 g/2 oz of the
       sultanas with mixed peel)
    Milk and sugar for glaze

If your yeast is not easy-blend then mix it with the warmed milk to which the caster sugar has been added. Otherwise, sieve the flour into a large bowl and add the dried yeast, a pinch of salt and the sugar. Make a well in the centre and gradually mix in the milk to make a soft but not sticky dough. If you have a food processor with a dough attachment you could use this to blend the dough together. Knead the dough with your hands for around 10 minutes or until it is elastic in texture. Grease a bowl and place the dough in it. Cover with cling film and place in a warm place to prove for one hour. The dough will approximately double in size.

Knead the dough again. Soften the butter and place half in the centre of the dough and fold the dough over it. Knead until the butter is thoroughly combined with the dough. Do the same with the other half of the butter. Knead in the fruit.

Shape the dough into a round shape and place on a baking sheet to rise for another hour.

Place in an oven preheated to 180°C/350°F/gas mark 4 for around 45 minutes. Remove and brush with the milk and sugar mixture to glaze and bake for approximately 20 minutes further. The bannock is cooked when it makes a hollow sound when the base is tapped and when it is golden brown all over.

PITCAITHLY BANNOCKS

Pitcaithly bannocks are basically shortbread with added mixed peel and nuts. A lower temperature is required to cook this than for ordinary shortbread to avoid scorching the preserved fruit.

150 g/6 oz plain flour
25 g/1 oz cornflour
75 g/3 oz caster sugar
100 g/4 oz butter
40 g/1½ oz preserved peel
40 g/1½ oz blanched almonds
40 g/1½ oz orange peel

Sieve the flour. Cream the butter and sugar together and gradually mix it with the flour. Chop the almonds and the peel very finely. Mix these ingredients with the shortbread dough. Roll the dough into a round that is about 20 cm/8 inches in diameter and score into eight segments. Prick the surface with a fork. Bake on a baking sheet at 150°C/300°F/gas mark 2 for around 50 minutes or until the shortbread turns golden but not brown. Transfer to a wire cooling tray and sprinkle with caster sugar.

SHORTBREAD

Shortbread is another iconic food that makes you immediately think of Scotland. Like steak pie, most people associate it with New Year celebrations. It takes a light touch to make truly good shortbread and the inclusion of semolina helps to give it the crunch and shortness it needs.

500 g/1 lb butter, softened
175 g/7 oz caster sugar
600 g/1¼ lb plain flour, sieved
   (crunchier biscuits can be made
   by substituting 50 g/2 oz
   semolina for 50 g/2 oz plain
   flour)

Preheat the oven to 160°C/325°F/gas mark 3. Beat together the butter and the sugar. Beat in the flour and semolina, 100 g/4 oz at a time, until smooth. If the dough becomes too stiff to stir, knead in the rest of the flour with your hands.

Grease and flour a large baking sheet (or a round shortbread mould). Roll out the dough and press into the baking sheet. Mark the dough into fingers or pie-shaped wedges and prick the pieces all over with the prongs of a fork. Bake in the centre of the oven for 30 to 40 minutes or until firm to the touch and delicately browned.

Makes about two dozen biscuits.

SODA LOAF

It's more traditional to use plain flour for this soda bread, but it is equally tasty, in fact in my opinion more so, if wholemeal flour is used. Try to mix with a light touch to keep as much air in the mixture as possible and don't knead the dough too much. Served straight from the oven with mature cheddar cheese and fresh butter, I can hardly think of anything nicer.

450 g/1 lb wholemeal flour
1 level tsp salt
1 level tsp baking soda
300 ml/generous ½ pint sour milk
   (or milk with 1 tbsp vinegar)

Preheat the oven to 200°C/400°F/gas mark 6. Sieve the flour, salt and baking soda into a bowl. Using a food mixer with a dough attachment will make the next stage easier, otherwise blend the sour milk with the flour mixture to make a soft dough rather like a scone dough, but don't let it become sticky.

   Place the dough in a loaf tin or shape into a round and score the top into eight sections. Cook for around 30 to 40 minutes.

POTATO SCONES

Potato scones are great freshly made and spread with butter, or fried as part of the great Scottish fry-up, or toasted the day after baking.

450 g/1 lb mashed potatoes
60 g/2½ oz plain flour
25 g/1 oz butter
½ tsp salt

Mash the potatoes thoroughly and make sure there are no lumps. Add the butter and salt to the potatoes. Sieve the flour and, very lightly, work it into the potato mixture with the butter. This is probably most easily done in a food processor because it is best if you handle it as little as possible. Cover a worksurface with flour and roll out the mixture thinly and cut into triangle shapes.

Heat a griddle or thick-bottomed frying pan and grease it lightly. Heat the scones for around 3 minutes on each side until browned.

CHITTERIN' BITES

* a chitterin' bite is a
sweet treat you
would give
yourself when
it's cold
(chitterin')

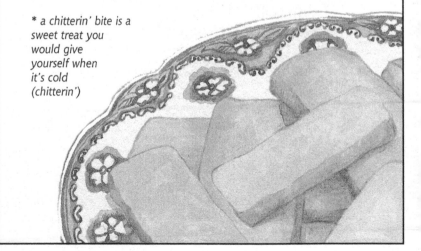

CARAMEL SHORTBREAD

I can't think of anything more fattening. So, frankly, what better reason to make what is also known in Scotland as Millionaire's Shortbread, presumably because of its rich ingredients. A favourite in tea rooms all over Scotland, it was also the best thing about Lanarkshire school dinners.

I have had divided reports about whether or not to pierce the can of condensed milk while it boils. While some have told me that it's perfectly safe, my 'O' grade physics, grade 3 tells me to avoid unnecessary risk of your kitchen being covered by exploding, caramelised, condensed milk by piercing the can.

Shortbread:
200 g/8 oz plain flour
100 g/4 oz semolina
1 tbsp self raising flour
150 g/6 oz caster sugar
250 g/10 oz butter, unsalted or
   slightly salted

Topping:
1 large tin condensed milk
   (400 g/14 oz)
200g/7 oz 70% cocoa or good
   quality milk chocolate

The day before you make the shortbread, place a tin of condensed milk, pierced at the top, in a pan of water, bring to the boil and cook over a medium heat for two hours. Remove from the heat and leave overnight to cool completely.

The next day make the shortbread as follows. Sieve the flour and mix lightly with the sugar. Cut the butter into cubes, straight from the fridge, and rub into the flour with the fingertips till the mixture looks like breadcrumbs. Make sure your hands are cold when you do this. Alternatively, attach the metal cutting blades to your food mixer and whiz all the ingredients together until they are combined. Pour the breadcrumbs into a rectangular shallow tin and press down using a pallet knife till the surface is flat. Don't be too heavy as it's preferable for the biscuit base to be crumbly. Bake for 40 minutes in an oven preheated to 150°C/300°F/gas mark 2.

Open the tin of condensed milk which should have turned thick and brown, and once the biscuit base has cooled, spread the caramel over it. Melt the chocolate over a bain marie, that is, in a glass bowl over a pot of simmering water, or in the microwave and spread over the caramel. Slice before it is completely cool, then leave in a cool place for the toppings to set.

EDINBURGH ROCK

This recipe won't make rock exactly the same as you can buy in the shops – it may be somewhat less soft and crumbly than the bought variety – but it's fun to make. Please make sure that you wait until the sugar mixture is cool enough to handle before you start rolling.

    450 g/1 lb sugar
    150 ml/¼ pint water
    ¼ tsp cream of tartar
    Green or yellow food colouring
    Peppermint or lemon flavouring
    A little oil

Pour the sugar into a thick-bottomed saucepan and pour the water over. Mix the sugar and water together and then turn on the heat to medium under the pan. Heat until the sugar has dissolved. Turn the heat up and, just before boiling point, add the cream of tartar. Boil the mixture until it reaches 'hard ball' consistency. You can use a sugar thermometer for this. When it reaches 120ºC/250ºF it is ready. Or, into a glass of cold water, drop a little of the mixture and when it forms a hard ball you will know that it has reached the correct temperature.

If you want, divide the mixture into two batches

so that you can colour and flavour them separately. Stir in the colourings and flavourings, pour them into two oiled baking tins and leave the mixtures to cool to a temperature that allows you to handle them. When cool enough to do so, pull and fold the mixtures several times. When it looks like you have trapped quite a lot of air into the sugar you can roll it into a long log shape and cut into small lozenges. Leave to cool completely and store in an air-tight box.

HELENSBURGH CANDY

This should turn out like a cross between fudge and tablet, according to my mum. Whether it was meant to turn out like this, I'm not entirely sure.

> 1 large tin of evaporated milk
>   (400 g/14 oz)
> 1.1kg/2½ lb sugar
> 50 g/2 oz butter
> ½ tsp vanilla essence

Place the milk, sugar and butter in a large, heavy pot. Heat this very slowly until the sugar has dissolved and then bring to the boil. After this, simmer gently for around 25 to 30 minutes. Test the hardness of the candy by dropping a blob of it into a bowl of cold water. If it forms a soft ball it should be ready.

  Remove from the heat and add the half-teaspoon of vanilla essence and beat for around 8 to 10 minutes or until the mixture is thick and creamy. Pour into a shallow, buttered tray and mark into squares. Allow to cool and cut into squares when cold.

PEPPERMINT CREAMS

I'm not sure how traditionally Scottish peppermint creams are, but by virtue of their high sugar content, the Scottish sweet tooth and by their appearance in almost every Church and WRI recipe pamphlet I've ever seen, they are included here.

Whites of two medium eggs
200 g/8 oz icing sugar
Peppermint oil

Beat the eggs with a hand mixer and add the sieved icing sugar gradually also using a hand blender until the paste becomes too difficult for the mixer to mix. Make a well in the middle of the paste and drop in around three drops of peppermint oil. Knead this in with your hands. Knead in the rest of the icing sugar. Taste the paste and add more peppermint if required and knead through.

Roll out to around $1/2$ cm/$1/4$ inch thick and cut out round shapes with a cutter, alternatively pinch off small balls of the mixture and flatten them. Place in a cool place to harden and store in an airtight tin.

PUFF CANDY

This is simple to make and should look like golden honeycomb. You could, if you want, cover it in a layer of chocolate, or smash it up and use it as a topping for ice creams and desserts.

> 4 tbsps granulated sugar
> 2 tbsps golden syrup
> 1 tsp bicarbonate of soda

Prepare, by buttering a baking tray.

Heat the syrup and the sugar in a heavy-bottomed saucepan, over a low heat. Stir the mixture well. Turn it up very slightly and watch for the formation of bubbles. When you see the bubbles, turn the heat down again and simmer for around 3 or 4 minutes. The sugar will become darker in colour.

Don't allow it to become too dark, remove from the heat when it is a golden brown and stir in the teaspoon of bicarbonate until the mixture froths up. Immediately pour this onto the buttered baking tray and leave to cool completely. Cutting this mixture out of the tray is not really possible so just hit it with a toffee hammer or a rolling pin once completely cool. Dip the pieces in chocolate or crush and use as a topping for ice-cream.

RAB'S HIGHLAND TOFFEE

This is another recipe from my mum, this time, her dad Robert's recipe for toffee. The mixture is barely stirred at all. A good, non-stick, thick-bottomed pot is therefore essential, and definitely don't go off and leave the room while you do something else.

> 1 large tin condensed milk
>   (400 g/14 oz)
> 2 tbsps golden syrup
> 1 tbsp vinegar
> Good quality butter for greasing tin

Melt the syrup and condensed milk together, add the vinegar and bring to the boil. Once it has reached the boil, simmer uncovered for 30 minutes. Do not stir the mixture.

Thoroughly grease a shallow tray with butter. After the 30 minutes are up, test the toffee by dropping a little blob into a bowl of cold water. If it is firm then it is ready. Pour into your greased tray and leave to cool thoroughly. Don't attempt to cut it into strips, wait till it is completely cold and smash it with a toffee hammer.

MACAROON BARS

It's almost worth making these just for the look on your recipients' faces when you tell them that this sweet treat was made with ... mashed potato! In truth, you would never know this. However, I remember buying some home-made macaroon bars from a Girls' Brigade troop who probably hadn't got their cookery badges. There were uncooked lumps of mashed potato throughout. Yum.

> 1 large floury potato, cooked and
>   mashed (very smoothly mashed!)
> Approx 500 g/1 lb icing sugar
> A large bar of chocolate, melted for
>   coating
> Toasted dessicated coconut

Boil the potato for 20 minutes and then mash very smoothly indeed. Using a food mixer, mix in a little icing sugar at a time, until it turns into a firm dough. Pinch off a piece of the dough and taste to ensure that you have included enough sugar. It should not taste of potato. If it does, add a spoonful of water and more icing sugar. Press into a tray and cut into bars. When set firmly, coat the bars in melted chocolate and then dip in toasted dessicated coconut.

TABLET

My Uncle Jimmy always made the best tablet. It takes a strong arm to keep the mixture stirred thoroughly without sticking while it boils on the stove, and then to beat the mixture thoroughly in its final stages. These days we have the good fortune to have food mixers and beaters to do this job. The wooden spoon that Jimmy used for beating it eventually wore away to a stump. My mum reckons that the tiny pieces of wood that must have gradually worn off added to its flavour. I remember what seemed to be huge slabs of it, wrapped in greaseproof paper (I'm told by my Aunt Jean that this was actually draughtsman's tracing paper!), so sweet it would last you for a week. It was usually made with the purpose of being sold for charity and was always a winner. It was probably a good thing that it sold out so quickly.

Other recipes for tablet include a teaspoon of vanilla extract but this one never did.

125 g/4 oz salted butter (butter
   with strong flavour is best)
1 kg/2¼ lb granulated sugar
1 cup full-cream milk
400 g/14 oz tin of condensed milk

Over a low heat, melt the butter in a very large, heavy-bottomed saucepan. Add the sugar and milk to this mixture and keep stirring until the sugar has dissolved. Add the condensed milk, turn the heat up a little and bring to the boil very slowly. After it reaches boiling point turn the heat down a little and allow the mixture to simmer for around 20 minutes. You should test the mixture for hardness after 18 minutes by dropping a little of the mixture from the spoon into a bowl of cold water. If the mixture turns into a soft ball that you can pick up between your fingers then it is time to remove the mixture from the heat. The mixture should also be slightly dark. But it's not finished yet.

Take off the heat and beat thoroughly for 3 to 5 minutes. Do not beat for longer than this or the mixture will start to crystallise. Pour into a shallow baking tray and score into fingers before it cools.

JAMS AND PRESERVES

ORANGE MARMALADE

It is said that marmalade originated as the remedy that Mary Queen of Scots' French chef made for her to tempt her to eat following an illness, hence the name is reputed to be derived from 'Mary Malade'.

> 2.25 kg/5 lbs oranges
> 4 litres/8½ pints of water
> 3.1 kg/7 lb sugar
> Butter

Wash the oranges thoroughly. Put them in a very large pot. Add 8 pints of water and bring to the boil, cover, then simmer for around 1 hour or until you are sure that the fruit is soft. Drain the oranges but do not throw the liquid away.

Allow the fruit and liquid to cool and then cut it into quarters. Using a serrated spoon, scoop out the orange flesh then remove, but reserve, the pips. Take the orange skins and remove as much pith as you can, but also reserve this. Put the pips and pith into a pan and simmer in 250 ml/½ pint of water for about 20 minutes. This liquid will help to set the marmalade. Strain it and add it to the orange flesh. Cut the orange peel as finely as you want and add it to the water the oranges were boiled in.

Grease a jelly pan or a large thick-bottomed pot with some butter. Measure the fruit pulp, peel and liquid for volume and for every 500 ml/1 pint add 450 g/1 lb of sugar. Add liquid and sugar to the pan and over a low heat melt all of the sugar.

When this has melted, bring the mixture to the boil. Boil and stir continuously. You might want to cover your hand and wrist with an oven glove or tea towel as the mixture will bubble and spit. Test if the mixture has set, after around 20 minutes by drizzling a little onto a chilled plate. Place your finger at the edge of the drizzle and slide it through. If the marmalade surface wrinkles then the mixture has reached the right consistency. Keep boiling if the marmalade does not wrinkle and test again after around 5 minutes.

To sterilise jars, wash in hot soapy water, dry and leave in a cool oven (150°C/300°F/gas mark 1–2), for 10 minutes.

Allow the marmalade to stand for 15 minutes and then pour into the sterlised jars.

RASPBERRY JAM

Straightforward to make, completely delicious, and all the more satisfying if you pick your own Scottish raspberries.

2 kg/4 lb Scottish raspberries
2 kg/4 lb sugar

Add the fruit to a jelly pan and warm on a low heat until the juice start to run. Add the sugar to the fruit and stir until it dissolves. Bring to the boil and test regularly to see if it has set. You do this by chilling a plate in the fridge for a few minutes then drizzling a little of the jam onto the plate. Wait for a few seconds, then draw your finger across the surface of the jam and if it wrinkles then the jam has reached its setting point. Sterilise some jam jars in the oven (see page 177).

Allow the mixture to cool slightly for around 15 minutes. Pot the jam in the warm jars. Serve with fresh scones or Scotch pancakes.

RHUBARB AND GINGER JAM

Not only is this jam absolutely delicious on hot scones or pancakes, but a dollop in the centre of hot creamy porridge is just gorgeous.

3 kg/7 lb rhubarb
3 kg/7 lb sugar
1 lemon
900 g/2 lb crystallised ginger

Wash the rhubarb and cut into small pieces. Put this in alternate layers with the sugar into a large earthenware pot (a 'crock' in Scots). Squeeze the lemon and pour the juice into the pot and leave this overnight. The next day there should be a good amount of liquid that has seeped from the rhubarb. Drain this off into a jelly pan and boil it with the preserved ginger for around 15 minutes. Then add the rhubarb and boil for a further fifteen minutes.

After this time remove from the heat, skim any scum from the surface of the pot and after around 15 minutes cooling time pour into jam jars that you have sterlised (see page 177).

CLYDE VALLEY CHUTNEY

The Clyde Valley was, and to an extent still is, a great area for buying farm produce straight from the farm or farm shop, or for picking your own fruit and vegetables. In summer you could easily have purchased all the fruits listed here along that stretch of the Clyde.

900 g/2 lbs Clydeside red tomatoes
900 g/2 lbs Clydeside Bramley apples
900 g/2 lbs Clydeside Victoria plums
900 g/2 lbs onions
450 g/1 lb sultanas
50 g/2 oz root ginger, grated
½ tsp powdered mace
½ tsp mixed spice
½ tsp cayenne pepper
450 g/1 lb demerara sugar
500 ml/1 pint vinegar
2 cloves garlic, chopped or crushed
1 tbsp salt (or less depending on
    personal taste)

Chop the tomatoes, apples and onions. Remove the stones from the plums and quarter them. Place them in a large pot or jelly pan with the sultanas. Grate the ginger, chop the garlic and add to the pan. Add all of the other ingredients and bring gently to the boil. Simmer for an hour. Cool, and pour into sterilised jars (see page 177).

GREEN TOMATO CHUTNEY

At the end of the season, what better way to avoid wasting unripened tomatoes than to turn them into a tangy chutney.

900 g/2 lbs green tomatoes
450 g/1 lb cooking apples
50 g/1 oz mixed spice
450 g/1 lb raisins
1 tbsp salt (or less if preferred)
450 g/1 lb onions
2 chillies
450 g/1 lb brown sugar
750 ml/1½ pints malt vinegar

Chop the tomatoes, apples and chillies finely and add together with all the ingredients to a very large pot or jelly pan. Bring to the boil and simmer for an hour. Cool and pour into sterlised jars (see page 177).

SPECIAL PICKLED ONIONS

This is another of my Aunt Isa's recipes. It uses sliced, large sweet onions rather than small pickling onions. They are spicy and seriously addictive.

2.25 kg/5 lbs large onions
¾ cup sugar
1 level tsp Jamaica pepper
1 level tsp cayenne pepper
1 level tsp ground ginger
500 ml/1 pint white malt vinegar
Salt

Peel the onions and slice into rings. Place the onions in layers in a large bowl, and between each layer give them a light sprinkling of salt. In a saucepan, boil the vinegar, sugar and spices and pour over the onions. Leave this for 24 hours, then strain off, but reserve, the liquor and pack the onions into sterilised jars (see page 177). Boil up the liquor and, while hot, pour over the onion. While still hot, put lids on the jars and leave for one week.

MUSHROOM KETCHUP

The recipe for mushroom ketchup in my Aunt Isa's notebook includes the sentence: 'Mushrooms for this purpose must be picked when its dry'. I remember often picking wild mushrooms with my dad in the fields around Carluke. If the weather had been just right we could end up gathering huge bags of them. This of course is not recommended if you do not know what you are looking for. Isa also recommended you use less salt than this recipe suggests, so do taste the juice in the recipe's second stage before adding more.

> 1.4 kg/3½ lbs mushrooms
> 50 g/2 oz salt
> A further 25g/1 oz salt per 150 ml/¼
>   pint of juice
> 5 cloves
> 7 g/¼ oz root ginger
> 7 g/¼ oz peppercorns
> Pinch of cayenne pepper

Break the mushrooms up into small pieces, place in a stoneware pan and sprinkle with salt. Let them stand for three days, frequently stirring and mashing them to cause the juice to flow. Strain and get all the juice possible from the mushrooms by adding pressure. To each quart of juice add 25 g/1 oz salt. Put the spices in a bag and boil with the mushrooms and juice for an hour, then strain. Bottle and cork, and use as a seasoning instead of salt.

DRINKS

GAELIC COFFEE

What better way to block out the winter chills or finish off a dinner party?

> ¾ cup hot filter coffee
> 1 ½ tsp brown sugar
> 1 large measure Scotch whisky or
>   whisky liqueur such as Drambuie
> 1 ½ tsp double cream (or more if
>   you like)

Warm a glass with hot water to prevent it cracking, then throw out the water. Refill the glass with boiling water then throw out the water again. Pour the coffee into the glass until just over half full and add sugar to taste. Stir thoroughly then add the whisky. Stir once more. Pour the cream over the back of a spoon so that it floats on top.

Serves one. Lightly whipped single cream can be used if you prefer it to double.

INDEX